NIGERIA

TITLES IN THE MODERN NATIONS OF THE WORLD SERIES INCLUDE:

Austria
Brazil
Canada
China
Cuba
Egypt
England
Ethiopia
Germany
Greece
Haiti
India
Ireland
Italy
Japan
Jordan
Kenya
Mexico
Nigeria
Norway
Peru
Poland
Russia
Saudi Arabia
Scotland
Somalia
South Africa
South Korea
Spain
Sweden
Switzerland
Taiwan
The United States
Vietnam

NIGERIA

BY SALOME NNOROMELE

LUCENT BOOKS
P.O. BOX 289011
SAN DIEGO, CA 92198-9011

On cover: Open-air market in Ibadan, Nigeria

Library of Congress Cataloging-in-Publication Data

Nnoromele, Salome, 1967–
    Nigeria / by Salome Nnoromele.
        p.   cm. — (Modern nations of the world)
    Includes bibliographical references and index.
    ISBN 1-56006-762-4 (hardback : alk. paper)
    1. Nigeria—Juvenile literature.   [1. Nigeria.]   I. Title.   II. Series.
DT515.22 .N6   2002
966.9—dc21

00-011642

CONTENTS

INTRODUCTION
NIGERIA: A COMPLEX SOCIETY

When Harry Land, a political scientist, described Nigeria as a very complex society, he was not exaggerating. Most people who live in modern Nigeria or who are familiar with its history would agree that the statement accurately defines the nation's historical and contemporary state of political and social affairs.

Nigeria is home to 250 to 450 ethnic groups who speak as many mutually exclusive languages, most with dialects. These groups, of which the major ones are the Hausas, the Fulanis, the Yorubas, and the Ibos, have different customs, adhere to different religious practices and beliefs, and for the most part have different outlooks on life.

NIGERIA'S MULTICULTURAL HERITAGE
The diversity of Nigeria's peoples has been a mixed blessing. On one hand, the country's multiethnicity has been responsible for a rich multicultural heritage, felt most profoundly in art, music, and literature, as well as in food and clothing. But on the other hand, the same ethnic diversity responsible for Nigeria's vibrant art and culture has also been the root of political trauma for the nation. Next to its art, Nigeria is perhaps best known for its political instability. Michael Crowder writes in *A Short History of Nigeria* that the union of the regions that make up the country "has covered such widely differing groups of peoples that not only the British who created it, but the inhabitants themselves have often doubted whether it could survive as a political entity."[1]

In fact, when Nigeria achieved independence from Britain on October 1, 1960, its new leaders inherited a divided nation. Because the Hausa and Fulani groups in the north had historically rejected Western education, very few of their people were qualified to participate effectively in the administration of the new independent state. They therefore feared

political and economic domination by the Western-educated Yorubas and Ibos in the south. For their part, the groups in the south were equally afraid of the power that the northerners' sheer numbers gave them. Then there was the question of minority groups. The minority groups had been completely neglected during British rule and increasingly demanded that their needs be addressed in the newly independent nation.

Since Nigeria's independence, the country has been unable to transcend these ethnic rivalries. The political power

Nigeria's cultural diversity has generated both a rich artistic tradition and a storm of political unrest.

struggles between the northern and southern components even resulted in a civil war. Compounding the problem of ethnic tensions are widespread corruption and governmental inefficiency. Many political leaders who pledged to serve and lead the country to economic prosperity have failed to develop Nigeria's economic resources and sometimes embezzled public funds.

This political instability and mismanagement of the country's resources have had tremendous effects on the social and economic lives of the people. Although Nigeria is the sixth largest producer of crude oil and petroleum in the world, it ranks as the thirteenth poorest nation. Unemployment stands at 28 percent, and about one-third of the population lives below poverty level.

The complexities of modern Nigeria continue to challenge its leaders. In May 1999, the military, which had ruled the country for twenty-eight of the forty years since independence, handed control to a democratically elected civilian government. The new administration under Olusegun Obasanjo has vowed to stamp out corruption and to foster unity and economic growth. Most experts, however, admit that the work facing the new administration is momentous. A special report published in the *New York Times* aptly summarizes the challenge: "As he tries to restore freedom and bring some measure of Nigeria's wealth to its overwhelming poor people, Mr. Obasanjo must contend with secessionist tendencies, the spreading imposition of Muslim Law in the north, rampant corruption and decades of neglect of the infrastructure that should hold his country together."[2] Only time will tell whether Nigeria will rise above its problems.

A Land of Immense Geographic Variety

Nigeria's location on the western coast of Africa, between the Sahara Desert to the north and the Atlantic Ocean to the south, gives it a striking range of contrasting natural environments. On its northern border lies the republic of Niger; the republic of Chad borders its northeast; to the west lies the republic of Benin; and to the east and southeast is the republic of Cameroon. To the extreme south lies the Gulf of Guinea. The country covers an area estimated at 356,700 square miles (or 923,770 square kilometers). This makes it about four times the size of the United Kingdom and more than twice the size of California. Nigeria is the largest country in West Africa and the twelfth largest in Africa as a whole.

Within Nigeria's borders are four major geographic regions: the semiarid, savannah plains of the far north; the hills, mountains, and plateaus of the central region; the tropical rain forests of the south; and the lowlands of the coastal region. Each region is defined by a distinct landscape and the lifestyles of the people who live in it.

THE NORTHERN SAVANNAH

South of the border with Niger and extending as far as the towns of Sokoto and Kebbi in the west and Borno to the east lies the great savannah grassland of the northern region, home to the Hausa and Fulani ethnic groups. The land is close to the Sahara Desert, and therefore has a semiarid environment. Rainfall is low, averaging sixteen to forty inches per year. Vegetation consists of tall grasses, scattered shrubs, and desert trees, including baobab, shea, cacti, and locust bean trees. Despite its semiarid environment, the region is agriculturally productive. The vastness of the grassland allows the Fulani people to raise cattle on a large scale; most of the beef and dairy products consumed in Nigeria come from this region. The Fulani also produce skins and hides used to manufacture different types of leather, including

The northern savannah region of Nigeria, where these men are gathering sugarcane, is agriculturally productive despite its semiarid temperatures.

Moroccan leather, a soft, red hide prized for its fine texture. Various crops, especially peanuts, sorghum, and cotton, thrive and are grown in large quantities. Yams and cassava are also important crops. The peanuts and cotton grown here are major Nigerian exports.

THE HILLS AND MOUNTAINS OF THE CENTRAL REGION

South of the savannah plain, annual rainfall increases. Old crystalline rocks emerge in mountainous ranges, rising from about twenty-seven hundred feet to more than five thousand feet above sea level, to form the highlands of the middle belt region, the geographic heartland of Nigeria. The region covers the Jos and Bauchi plateaus, extending to the Mandara and Bamenda mountains at the border with Cameroon and the upper Niger and Benue valleys to the south. This makes the heartland the largest geographic region in the country.

The landscape is varied and scenic. The towering mountains of the Mandara and Bamenda areas look like a confused chain of massive rocks and are impressive and imposing. The rest of the heartland alternates between scattered hills and plateaus. Many winding rivers and huge waterfalls bisect the surfaces of the plateaus to create open flat valleys and deep gorges. During the rainy season, when the valleys and the mountains are carpeted with green grass, the views are spectacular. Rainfall averages between 50 and 60 inches per year, except in some parts of the Mandara and Bamenda regions, where more than 150 inches of rain fall annually. Vegetation consists of grasses and thickly wooded areas around the river valleys.

The region is home to many ethnic groups in Nigeria, including the Tivs, Igala, Nupe, and Idoma. Most of the people make a living by raising goats, sheep, and other livestock. They also raise crops, including yams, cassava, maize, cocoyams, plantains, potatoes, onions, tomatoes, beans, guinea corn, and millet in the valleys and along the ridges. But the rocky nature of the terrain makes large-scale farming difficult. Most farmers produce just enough food for their families.

The scarcity of good farmland, however, is compensated for by the region's abundance of mineral resources. Large deposits

In the mountains of Mandara and Bamenda, raising livestock accounts for much of the Nigerian livelihood.

of tin, iron, coal, gold, uranium, and columbite are mined to provide raw materials to many thriving industries located in the area. Both mining and industry provide good employment opportunities for local residents. Nigeria is the largest producer of columbite and the only producer of tin in Africa.

The region is rich in wildlife as well as mineral resources. Native wild animals include baboons, antelope, deer, monkeys, leopards, elephants, hyenas, and various species of exotic birds. Many of Nigeria's wildlife reserves, including its primary wildlife reserve, the Yankari Game Reserve, are located in the heartland. Hunting is a favorite recreational activity among the natives. "Bush meat," that is, meat from wild animals, is considered a delicacy and supplements the plant foods in the natives' diet.

THE TROPICAL RAIN FOREST BELT

The mountains and highlands of the central region gradually descend southward from the upper Niger-Benue valley to the lower plains of the southern region. The region is known as the tropical rain forest belt because of the high amount of rain it receives, and the density of its vegetation and high forest trees. Annual rainfall varies from 80 inches in the southwest to 125 inches in the east. Temperatures range between 70 degrees and 90 degrees Fahrenheit. Humidity is high and increases toward the coast. There are three distinct zones of the rain forest region: the cocoa belt of Yorubaland, the high

A VARIED LANDSCAPE

Anthropologist Lois Mitchison describes the varied landscape of Nigeria in her book *Nigeria, Newest Nation.*

To the air traveler flying into Nigeria from the north, it is a country in contrasting layers. The first layer is desert, getting greener and more cultivated as the Sahara is left behind; further south, more trees in the rolling orchard country of the Savannah; and then a dense green carpet of forest broken occasionally by the sudden flash of a flowering creeper or by ribbons of roads or sluggish looking green-brown rivers. Near the coast, the tall trees give way to a low swampy growth, mostly of mangroves. The final coast line is sand beaches with Atlantic surf breaking them.

forests of Bini land in the southwest, and the palm forest belt of Iboland in the southeast.

The cocoa belt lies in the upper level of the southwest. As a result of settlement patterns and deforestation, the area's vegetation consists mostly of tall grasses, although patches of densely wooded areas are found around the many rivers and streams here. The weather is cool and the soil claylike, making the area particularly favorable for the cultivation of cocoa. Even though other products such as citrus fruits, coffee, rubber, palm, and kola nuts are grown in the region, cocoa is by far the leading crop. Cocoa was introduced in the latter part of the nineteenth century, and since then its production has become the area's primary industry. More than 150,000 tons of cocoa are exported every year, making Nigeria the third largest producer of cocoa in the world, after Ghana and Brazil.

South of the cocoa belt lies the heart of the Nigerian rain forest, known as Bini land. The whole area is enclosed by extensive blocks of luxuriant high forests. Grass is generally absent, and the region is richly endowed with such massive tropical trees as the iroko, oil bean, rubber, mahogany, silk cotton, walnut, and sapele wood. Much of the rubber and timber produced in Nigeria, both for export and local uses, comes from Bini land. The region is home to 95 percent of the sawmill, plywood, timber, and logging industries in Nigeria. Its location close to the coast makes the transportation of timber efficient.

The southeastern zone of the tropical rain forest contains the palm belt of Iboland. Here, high temperatures and humidity favor quick plant growth, and crops such as yams, cocoyams, maize, peanuts, and different types of vegetables and fruits thrive. Rice is grown in areas nearer to the coast. But the palm belt takes it name from the predominance of oil palm trees that grow wild in its forests or are cultivated in plantations.

Oil palms are very tall and look like coconut trees. But instead of coconuts, they produce clusters of small, red fruits that are saturated with oil. The oil is the most significant export crop of the region. Since the nineteenth century, palm oil has been exported to other parts of Nigeria and the world; it is used for cooking as well as for making household goods such as soap, margarine, and body lotions.

Rice makes a favorable crop in the palm belt of Iboland where humidity and temperatures are high.

THE COASTLINE

The last geographic region is the coastline. Nigeria boasts 530 miles of coastline, stretching from about twelve miles outside the city of Lagos in the west through the Niger Delta to the border with Cameroon. Land is slightly above sea level, rising as one moves inland. The coastline consists of a network of swamps, creeks, and lagoons intersected by sandbanks. The whole area is covered by thick forests of red mangroves and raffia palms.

In the middle of the coastline lies the Niger Delta, riddled with an intricate system of natural water channels through which the Niger River empties into the sea. From the fifteenth through the early twentieth century, the delta provided the largest number of sheltered port sites along the coastline of West Africa, including such historic ports as Bonny, Warri, Brass, and Forcados. In the sixteenth through the eighteenth century, the combined trade of these ports made the Niger Delta the most important slave market along the West African coast, and in the early part of the nineteenth century, when palm oil became the main item of trade, these ports exported more palm oil than the other countries of West Africa combined.

Today the Niger Delta is known for its numerous oil wells. First discovered in 1956, the petroleum produced in the region forms Nigeria's primary export—and the chief source of its revenue. But because the land on which the oil is found is owned by the government, not by individuals, the natives have not benefited much from the oil pumped from their

THE NIGER

In his book *History of Nigeria,* Alan Burns describes the great Niger River, one of the major physical features of Nigeria, and the one from which the country takes its name.

The Niger rises in the mountains to the north-east of Sierra Leone, about 150 miles from the sea [the Atlantic Ocean], and flows in a north-easterly direction till it reaches Timbuktu. From this point it flows eastward for about 200 miles, and then flows in a south-easterly direction to the town of Lokoja [in southwestern Nigeria], about 340 miles from the sea. Here it receives the waters of its principal tributary, the Benue, on its left bank, and from here it flows due south to a point a few miles below [the town of] Abo, where the delta commences. This delta extends along the coast for over 100 miles, and for about 140 miles inland; the river here forms an intricate network of channels, dividing and subdividing, and a multitude of creeks connect these branches of the Niger not only with one another but also with other rivers. . . . The length of the Niger is 2,600 miles of which about two-thirds lie outside Nigeria, and the area of the river basin is estimated to exceed 500,000 square miles.

The Niger River runs northeast from the mountainous area of Sierra Leone to the city of Timbuktu.

region. Life for most of the people is the same as it has been for generations. There are no good roads; the many creeks and thick mangrove swamps have made the construction of roads difficult. Travel is mostly by boats and canoes. Houses are built on stilts to protect them against frequent floods. The people make a living by fishing and trading.

CLIMATE

Because Nigeria is close to the equator, its climate is hot. Average temperatures range from an absolute minimum of 60 to 110 degrees Fahrenheit. However, the differences in physical features from north to south make the northern climate hotter and drier than in the south. The south is more humid, especially near the coast.

Nigeria has two seasons: wet and dry. The rainy season runs from March to September, and the dry season lasts from October to February. Along the coast, however, it rains even during the dry season, but not as much as during the rainy season. The beginning of the rainy season brings violent rainstorms that uproot trees, destroy houses, and cause flooding, especially in deforested areas. Farmers usually wait until after the first rains to start planting to reduce the chances that young seedlings will be destroyed by the storms. The dry season is cooler than the wet season and is accompanied by a phenomenon known as the harmattan. The harmattan is a cold, dry, dusty wind that comes from the Sahara Desert. During the harmattan, the nights and early mornings are especially cold and dry, and dense fogs limit visibility. Even though it never gets cold enough to wear winter coats and jackets, people wear sweaters to keep warm and cover themselves with thick blankets to sleep comfortably at night. In the north, sandstorms and bushfires are common. Smog and soot from burning bushfires are as much a part of the harmattan as its dry chilly weather.

A man stands next to an oil-drilling well in the oil-rich region of the Niger Delta.

NATURAL RESOURCES

Nigeria's varied landscape and good climate result in many natural resources. Much of the country receives a large amount of rain, which

THE HARMATTAN

Although global warming has taken the edge off the harmattan, Ronald Miller, a British geographer in Nigeria, describes its unpleasant effects in his essay "The Climate of Nigeria."

The Harmattan is often spoken of as the redeeming feature in the climate of Nigeria and indeed West Africa. True, it has one good feature—it brings cold nights; one snuggles into bed under three blankets and probably gets better sleep and therefore more rest than at some other seasons, but the air can often feel just as cool in rainy weather. The excessively low humidity of the Harmattan is on almost every count a bad property. It is uncomfortable; it first attacks the mucus of the nose and throat and in some people may cause a catarrh [respiratory ailment] which lasts till the air recovers humidity. With lower humidity, the lips, skin, and even finger-nails crack. The load of dust which the Harmattan brings from the interior of the continent makes everything filthy and the sky becomes dull and oppressive as on a "November" day in Britain. . . . In the plant world, Harmattan is comparable to frost in higher latitudes, blighting, checking and even entirely destroying growth. It has a secondary effect, too, in that it greedily evaporates all available water and so dissipates much of the precious stock of moisture held in the soil over which a crust may form which no ordinary hoe can deal with. Leather, paper, wood and even plastics suffer from the extreme desiccation; woodwork comes apart at the joints and many even collapse, and all kinds of inconvenience and expense may be caused by warping. Poor qualities of paper become brittle and may disintegrate like a piece of newspaper scorched in front of a fire.

means that it is blessed with rich farmlands, enabling the people to effectively produce food for local consumption and export. Its coastal waters provide an abundance of different types of fish, and it also has extensive forest reserves and large deposits of mineral resources. If these economic resources are well maintained and managed, Nigeria could become one of the richest nations in the world. But it has been plagued by chronic political instability and corrupt political leaders who mismanage public funds and exploit ethnic differences for private gains.

2

THE PEOPLE AND THEIR HERITAGE

Nigeria is often called the "giant of Africa" because it is the most populous country on the continent. Its current population is estimated at 113 million, and is at least double that of Egypt, the second most populous African nation. Roughly one in every four Africans is a Nigerian.

Nigeria also contains the most ethnic variety of any African country. There are believed to be up to 450 distinct ethnic groups. Some groups consist of as few as five hundred members, while others exceed 20 million. The predominant ones are the Hausas, the Fulanis, the Yorubas, the Binis, and the Ibos. These groups speak different languages, many with dialects; have different histories; and, for the most part, practice different religions. Prior to their contact with Europe, these groups had developed elaborate kingdoms, empires, and city-states and had lived independent of each other for centuries. Today, they still live in the same lands they have occupied for hundreds of years, and their different cultural heritages have combined to make Nigeria a dynamic society.

THE HAUSAS

Living in northern Nigeria are the Hausas, estimated at 21 million. They speak the Hausa language, one of the major languages spoken in Africa today, even outside Nigeria. Because the language is simple, musical, and contains a rich vocabulary, it is one of the two African languages most frequently taught in universities around the world. (The other language is Swahili.) Scholars date the Hausas' arrival in Nigeria at about the tenth century A.D. when a group left their home in North Africa and wandered south across the Sahara Desert. There they settled among the original inhabitants, whose history has not survived, and in time absorbed and displaced them.

The Hausas lived in small village communities. However, by the fourteenth century, many of the villages had grown into towns and cities and a few combined to form centralized

A young Hausa girl sits among members of her community.

city-states. The major ones, known as the Hausa Bakwai (the authentic seven), were Duara, Kano, Katsina, Rano, Gobir, Garun Gabas, and Zazzau (present-day Zaria). These city-states are said to have been developed by—and bear the names of—the seven sons of the original Hausa ancestor, Abu Yazid, who led the group from North Africa to the region.

Kings ruled the Hausa states with the help of a council made up of important men in society, men with wealth as well as military abilities. The council members were responsible for collecting taxes, mostly on land and cattle, and training and maintaining the state army. Having an effective army was important because, even though the states claimed a common ancestry, their rulers waged wars against each other. A king and his council had the responsibility of protecting their city against invasion. Massive walls built of sun-baked clay were used to fortify towns and villages

THE TOWN OF KANO

The town of Kano in Hausaland has historically been a great commercial crossroads. Colin Latchem, in his book *Looking at Nigeria*, states that the heart of the city still retains its ancient atmosphere, even though the areas around it, known as New Kano, enjoy modern industry and commerce.

> Today there is a modern industrial and commercial area outside the old city and [New] Kano is a central point for road, rail and international air routes. The old city [called Old Kano] is a red-brown labyrinth of alleys, courtyards and boxlike houses. The narrow streets are thronged with the tall, naturally elegant northerners. Street vendors, beggars, craftsmen and barbers gather under the few trees. Donkey trains laden with cotton, sugar cane and firewood are urged on by straw-hatted riders astride rear donkeys. Camels carry merchandise to and from one of the world's largest and oldest open-air markets. Some of the indigo-robed and veiled Tuareg who trek down from the desert on their camels stay to work in Kano as night-watchmen. Their fierce looks, swords, and spears are enough to deter the "thief men." Close to one of the old city gates, dyers squat around vile-smelling dye pits, dipping lengths of bunched cotton into blue indigo dye to make beautiful tie-and-dye cloth.

against this threat. The council also initiated war against a neighboring state, if necessary.

Although the Hausas were good farmers, their real love was trading. Because of their nearness to the Sahara, the Hausas could trade with North African merchants involved in trans-Saharan commerce. Many of the Hausa cities were at the base of the trade route, and merchants who frequently visited and traded with the locals helped the cities to develop into flourishing commercial centers. Kano, especially, acquired an international name, and many who visited the area wrote about it. They described a city walled around with thick mud, and a large central market where articles such as cloth, ivory, and spices could be bought. The city was also known for its dye. People as far away as Libya often sent cloth to Kano to be dyed. The Hausas maintained their way of life until the next wave of immigrants, the Fulanis, arrived.

The Fulanis

The Fulanis share a common history with the Hausas. This is why even though the two groups have distinct origins, most Nigerians consider them one political and religious entity. Numbering about 6 million, the Fulanis are the second largest group in northern Nigeria. The Fulanis migrated from northern Senegal around the twelfth century A.D., about two centuries after the Hausas had arrived and settled the land. The Fulani native tongue is Fulfulde, a language related to those spoken in Senegal, their original home.

The Fulanis were mostly pastoral nomads, raising cattle and sheep. When they arrived in Hausaland, the Hausas welcomed them for the milk, butter, and manure provided by their herds. Even though the Hausas remained the rulers, since land was available the Fulanis settled peacefully in the region. In time, they split into three distinct groups, who adopted different ways of life.

The Hausa people built the mud-walled city of Kano as a base for trading cloth, spices, and ivory with merchants from North Africa.

The first group, the Borroro Fulanis, remained herdsmen. They established themselves across the border between Nigeria and the republic of Niger. Following their traditional nomadic way of life, they moved from place to place with their herds of cattle, sheep, or goats in search of water and pasture. Their lives revolved around seasonal cycles. During the dry seasons, most migrated to the Niger-Benue valley, where water was available and animals could feed on the stubble of harvested crops; during the rainy season, they returned to the savannah grassland of their home at the border between Niger and Nigeria. The Borroro Fulanis' way of life was simple because of their nomadic existence. Their houses consisted of portable huts or temporary shelters made of branches and leaves so that they could be easily dismantled when it was time to move again. They owned few possessions—things like ropes, cooking pots, mats, blankets, knives, and tools necessary for their lifestyle. Dairy products, such as milk, butter, and cheese, were their staple food. They often sold or exchanged butter and milk for things they did not produce, such as rice, tea, and sugar. Today, the Borroro Fulani still sustain their nomadic lifestyle.

The second group of Fulanis, called the Fulani Siire, became primarily farmers. Originally nomads, they were forced to turn to farming after losing their cattle to disease or poor maintenance. They raised native crops such as millet and corn and lived in permanent communities.

The third group was the Fulani Gida. This group was semi-pastoral and combined farming and cattle raising. Very often the household was split: the male head of the family and the women would remain at home to tend the crops, while the younger married and unmarried sons would move with the herds. Today, this lifestyle pattern still continues among some Fulanis.

During the fourteenth century, about two centuries after the arrival of the Fulanis, a group of people from Senegal known as the Mandigos brought the Islamic religion into the Hausa-Fulani land. (Before this time, the people practiced the traditional African religion of belief in many gods.) Many of the Hausas and Fulanis, particularly the Fulani Siire and the Fulani Gida, converted to the new religion. The Borroro Fulanis, however, maintained their pre-Islamic beliefs and values. The introduction of Islam brought about a new class

A Fulani girl carries a pot. Though mostly nomadic, the Fulanis settled among the Hausas and eventually split into three distinct groups.

of Fulanis, the Torrobe Fulani. These were Muslims (followers of Islam) who devoted their lives to studying and teaching the values of the Islamic faith. In time, they were considered the professional class, the religious leaders of the people.

The Hausas remained the ruling class in the northern region until 1804, when Othman Dan Fodio began a jihad (an Islamic holy war) against the Hausa city-states. Dan Fodio was a Torrobe Fulani who felt that he was called by Allah (God) to institute Islamic principles in the land. He thought that the Hausa rulers were failing in their responsibility to govern according to Islamic laws. He noted that, although the Hausas had converted to Islam five hundred years before, the government still retained its pre-Islamic structure. He condemned what he called the lack of morality at court, particularly the fact that men and women were seen together in public, even though Islam requires the strict separation of the sexes. He also argued that Islam does not support the heavy cattle taxes the Hausa rulers demanded from the Fulani people.

Many Fulani people supported Dan Fodio's cause and joined his army intent on overthrowing the Hausa rulers. His crusade was so effective that by 1808, most of the Hausa states had been conquered and brought under his leadership. In 1809, Dan Fodio established his base in the town of Sokoto, at the northwestern part of Hausaland. In time, the whole region became known as the empire of Sokoto. Dan Fodio was known as the sultan, the commander of the faithful, to whom all owed allegiance. Under his rule, the Hausa towns retained their commercial environment, but their political institutions and way of life were adapted to suit the Islamic faith. The Hausa rulers were driven out and replaced by Fulani emirs or Islamic rulers who governed the Hausa towns with the help of a group of appointed officials. The officials were responsible for collecting taxes and for general administration, as in the past. But the judicial system was now based on strict Islamic laws known as the Shari'a. The judges, who were always Muslim scholars and leaders, decided criminal and civil suits according to Islamic beliefs.

Dan Fodio died in 1817, leaving the kingdom to his brother and son. Under their reign, the Sokoto empire extended its influence through Hausaland to the modern-day republics of Benin, Cameroon, and Niger. The empire remained powerful until the British army invaded Sokoto during the late nineteenth century.

THE YORUBAS

The Yoruba people form the third major ethnic group in Nigeria. They occupy the southwestern part of the country, and their history is as eventful as those of the Hausas and Fulanis in the north. The Yorubas are also found in other African countries such as Benin and Togo, but the majority

OTHMAN DAN FODIO AND THE FULANI JIHAD

In his book *Milestones in Nigerian History*, Nigerian historian J. F. A. Ajayi asserts that the jihad led by the Fulani Othman Dan Fodio in the early part of the nineteenth century was the first step toward uniting the peoples that make up modern Nigeria.

The most important theme of our history . . . has been the gradual process of unification. This process may, in a very real sense, be said to have begun in May 1804 when Shehu Uthman dan Fodio declared a jihad, or holy war, in Gobir in the north-west corner of Nigeria. Before then, we had the histories of the different people in Nigeria, sometimes overlapping, but by and large separate. The Fulani jihad was the first event of a truly nation-wide significance in our history. Hardly any part of the country entirely escaped its influence. Its effect was considerable on peoples as widely separated as the Yoruba, the Igala, and the Kanuri. Above all, it began to knit together inextricably the histories of the Fulani, the Hausa, the Gwari, the Nupe, the Jukun, and a host of other peoples in what is now Northern Nigeria.

Uthman dan Fodio was not seeking consciously to unify Nigeria. He was not even so much a fighting empire-builder as a religious reformer famous for his piety, his inspiring sermons, and his writings on Theology and Canon Law. He was a highly educated man who became a well-known teacher exhorting his students among others to follow the strict rules of the Quadiyya brotherhood of which he was himself a member. . . . Of course before the Fulani, other people in Nigeria had with varying degrees of success sought to create hegemonies [control] over as wide an area as possible. . . . But these older empires had little appeal outside their immediate metropolitan areas. They existed only as long as the metropolitan areas could maintain enough military force to keep the rest of the empire in place. As soon as there were any weaknesses at the center, the outlying districts tended to break away. Thus these older empires did not solve the problem of how to bind together various peoples in one state. The Fulani empire was not only larger than these, it was also more successful in keeping its different sections together.

live in Nigeria. They speak a language also known as Yoruba, which, like most other Nigerian languages, has many dialects. Seven distinct dialects represent the seven Yoruba groups: Ilesha, Ijebu, Ondo, Ekiti, Egba, Oyo, and Ogun. The Yorubas carve marks on their faces to indicate which group they come from. Although internal differences between the groups exist, they see themselves as one political and social entity in Nigeria.

According to legend, the first wave of the Yorubas arrived from North Africa, probably Egypt, around 200 A.D. They settled at a place called Ife before migrating to other parts of the southwest region. For this reason, the town of Ife is considered the birthplace of the Yorubas and the spiritual capital of the people. The little that is known about this period in Yoruba history has been deduced from the sculptures that have survived. The Ife sculptures, mostly bronzes, chronicle the lives of the different rulers and indicate that the people were highly skilled in metalworking and pottery making. The arts of this period are showcased in many museums around the world as a witness to this original culture.

This Yoruba man has facial markings to indicate which of the seven Yoruba groups he belongs to.

Between 600 and 1000 A.D., a second wave of immigrants led by Oduduwa and his son, Awranyan, came into the region. They conquered the original inhabitants, settled among them, and in time adopted their culture. Initially, the society was organized around small independent patrilineal villages. However, in the centuries that followed, most of the villages grew into towns and developed complex, centralized systems of government. Each of the towns was governed by a king, or *oba*, a descendant of the town's founder.

The *obas* ruled with the help of a council of chiefs, made up of representatives of the town's prominent families. Although the people had tremendous respect for the *oba*, his position was mostly ceremonial. The real power rested with the council of chiefs, the prime decision-making body of the town. The chiefs would meet daily in a palace courtyard to discuss issues and make decisions, which they

THE TOWN OF IFE

Historically, the town of Ife is considered sacred to the Yorubas. The people believe that this was the first place they settled before migrating to other parts of southwestern Nigeria. The famous Yoruba shrine, Orisha, is located in Ife, and followers make annual pilgrimages to worship there. The king of Ife (the *oni* of Ife) is seen as the symbolic father of all other Yoruba kings. Whenever a king is crowned, the *oni* of Ife must be invited. During the coronation ceremony, the *oni* has the honor of crowning the new king, a symbolic gesture of giving him authority to rule.

then sent to the *oba* for approval. The council of chiefs also acted as the highest judicial body and the final court of appeal. It heard both civil and criminal cases brought before it and helped resolve family disputes. Its decisions were considered final.

Structurally, the Yoruba towns looked like a spider's web or a wheel. Each town was enclosed by high walls, with the *oba*'s palace in the center. Every road in the town led to the palace. The palace was a big compound, thickly walled around with only one main gate. Inside, the palace contained many houses and interconnected courtyards where members of the royal family lived with their servants. Some palaces housed as many as a thousand people.

The town's market was situated in front of the palace, with the front courtyard connecting the palace to the market. Often, the *oba* sat in the front courtyard and watched the regular activities of the marketplace from a distance. This symbolized the *oba*'s role as the overseer of the people. Beyond the main town wall were the farmlands, and beyond the farmlands, outskirts that connected one town to another. Many of the Yorubas were farmers; few were traders or artisans.

Religion was an important aspect of life for the Yorubas, who believed in many gods. The supreme god, Oludumare, was believed to be the creator of the world. But he was not directly involved in the people's daily lives. The day-to-day aspects of life were thought to be controlled by the lesser gods, *orisha*, whose major functions were to protect and provide for the people. The Yorubas believed that the *orisha* were individuals who had lived on earth but, instead of dying,

This late eighteenth-century oba *statue represents a Nigerian community's ruler.*

achieved divinity because of their leadership and warrior skills. Diviners, known as *balawos,* acted as intermediaries between the gods and the people. Annual festivals were held to celebrate each of the gods.

THE YORUBA KINGDOM OF OYO

All the Yoruba towns sought to maintain their independence, but this was not always possible. Some towns with weak rulers were brought under the control of a more powerful ruler. The most prominent town to emerge in Yoruba history was Oyo. Oyo, in the northern part of Yorubaland, had been settled by Oduduwa, the leader of the second migrant group. His descendants developed the town into a prosperous commercial center, and in subsequent centuries they conquered neighboring towns.

By the twelfth century A.D., the king of Oyo, called the *alafin* of Oyo, ruled so many Yoruba towns that he formed the Oyo empire. In Ibadan, the capital of the Oyo empire, the *alafin* ruled with his council of seven chiefs, known as the Oyo Mesi. At its height, the Oyo kingdom extended its influence as far west as Benin, Togo, and Ghana. The original rulers of the conquered towns were allowed to retain their positions as long as they recognized the authority of the *alafin* of Oyo and sent annual tributes (taxes) to him. Much like the Fulani empire of Sokoto, the Oyo empire collapsed during the nineteenth century when the British brought the region under their control.

THE BENIN EMPIRE

Southeast of the Yorubas live another important ethnic group in Nigeria, the Binis (also called Beni or Benin). Because they share history with the Yorubas, many people often group the Bini and the Yoruba together. But they have a distinct cultural identity. The Bini people speak a language known as Edo, so they are sometimes referred to as Edo-speaking people.

According to legend, when the second wave of the Yorubas arrived in Nigeria, the son of their leader Oduduwa, Awranyan, journeyed with his men to a place a little southeast of where the rest of the group settled. There they befriended the original inhabitants and in time adopted the native culture. Awranyan was a strong leader. Gradually, he and his descendants established a monarchy with a capital at Benin City. By the twelfth century A.D., at the same time that the Yorubas' Oyo empire was emerging, the Benin empire was making its influence felt in the regions south of Yorubaland, around the Niger, and all the way through the towns of Asaba and Onitsha in the east and Lagos in the west.

The Bini government was much like that of Oyo. The *oba* ruled with the help of a seven-member council of chiefs. The chiefs were great warriors. Their primary duty was to ensure peace and stability in the kingdom and maintain a standing army both for waging wars and defending the kingdom.

When Portuguese merchants landed on the coast of West Africa in 1471 and stumbled upon Benin City, they were impressed. Their writings describe a kingdom walled round

A bronze head, created between the sixteenth and seventeenth centuries, depicts a member of the Benin ethnic group, also known as the Edo-speaking people.

with a huge mound of earth as tall and as wide as a two-story house. Outside the wall was a ditch as deep and as wide as the wall was high and thick. Inside the kingdom lived a vibrant people, mostly farmers. The king was deeply respected and worshiped as a god, the protector of his people. Like the Oyo empire, the Benin kingdom lasted until the nineteenth century, when internal divisions and pressures from European slave traders and colonists weakened it.

THE IBOS

The Ibos (also known as Igbos) constitute the last major ethnic group in Nigeria. Estimated at 16 million, they are the largest ethnic group in the south. The Ibos speak the Igbo language, which has many dialects that are not always understood by all Ibos. For example, while all Ibos understand and use central Ibo, only people from the Abakaliki region understand and use the Abakaliki dialect.

Unlike those of the Hausas, the Fulanis, the Binis, and the Yorubas, who claim North Africa as their original home, the origins of the Ibos are unknown. This is because the people did not develop the art of writing until the eighteenth century, and because legends that tell about the people's origin have not survived. However, archaeological evidence indicates that the Ibos have occupied their present land for a long time, probably since the ninth century A.D.

The Ibos structured their political lives differently from the Yorubas and the Hausas. The Yorubas have a saying that "a town without a king is no town," alluding to their monarchical form of government. The Ibos, on the other hand, say that in Iboland, "everyone is king," referring to their non-centralized, individualistic political structure. Except in a few communities such as Onitsha and Asaba that were influenced by the Benin empire, the Ibos never developed centralized governments with kings or chiefs. They established no kingdoms, empires, or city-states. They lived mainly in small democratic villages where decisions were made in consultation with every member of the community through established institutions, such as a council of elders, women's associations, age groups, and secret societies. Age and diligence were respected by the people, and elders who had achieved social status through industry were chosen to represent the interest of the people when dealing with outsiders.

THE NOK CULTURE

The first people to occupy present-day Nigeria (and as far as we know, West Africa) were the Nok people. The Nok culture flourished from 500 to 200 B.C. in what is today the middle belt (the heartland) of Nigeria in the highlands of Jos, Minna, Zaria, and the capital, Abuja. Except for the terra-cotta sculptures that archaeologists have discovered in various parts of their homeland, not much has survived from the Nok culture. Their artwork, however, reveals that the Nok people were highly sophisticated in their knowledge of ironwork and bronze. They were also pagans, practicing the traditional African religion of belief in many gods. By the time the Nok culture came to an end around 200 B.C., other parts of modern Nigeria were already occupied by the ancestors of the different ethnic groups that make up the country today.

The land formerly occupied by the Noks now contains an extreme variety of peoples, the greatest concentration of ethnic minorities in Nigeria. Grouped together, these minorities constitute a majority of the population. However, their fragmentation into small ethnic groups gives them their minority status. Members of these ethnic groups, which include the Tiv, Ijaw, Igala, and Nupe, adhere to the traditional African religion; some, however, are Christians, and a small minority are Muslims.

The Ibos were farmers. A family raised what it needed, and any surplus crop was sold to buy items the family did not produce. Men and women shared the responsibility for farming. Men cultivated mainly yams, the staple food for the Ibos. Women cultivated garden crops such as okra, tomatoes, peppers, cassava, and cocoyams; they also brought the yams home during harvest.

Religion was important to the Ibos, and, to a large extent, the foundation of traditional society. The Ibos practiced the traditional African belief in many gods, but they modified them according to their own reality. There was a supreme god, Chukwu, who created the world, and beneath him were a number of lesser gods, *agbala* or *arusi*, such as Amadioha (the god of thunder) and Ani (the god or goddess of the earth). Unlike in the Yoruba belief system, the deities were not humans who achieved divinity. They were nature gods, each responsible for controlling an aspect of nature. Their beginnings, much like that of the supreme god, were unfathomable.

Each village had its own protector god to whom it paid homage. The village gods were thought to control every aspect of life in the village. Prosperity was a reward for the good deeds of the people; failure and hardship resulted from the anger of the gods. The people, therefore, worked to live in harmony with nature to avoid bringing the anger of the gods upon them. Priests and priestesses represented the people before the gods, and each village held an annual festival in honor and celebration of its god.

The arrival of the British during the eighteenth century brought changes to the Ibo belief systems and ways of life. British missionaries introduced Christianity, and the Ibos converted en masse to the new religion. Today it is estimated that as many as 90 percent of Ibos are Christians of various denominations, with Catholics in the majority. Ten percent of the Ibos still hold fast to traditional religion, and a good number have found ways to combine traditional values with the Christian faith.

Colonization by the British brought Nigeria's different ethnic groups together to form one political entity. But each group has maintained many of its unique traditional values and ways of life. Often, the differences in cultural values have resulted in ethnic divisions and conflicts, but the mix of the different peoples creates a dynamic and intriguing social and political climate.

CONTACT WITH EUROPE

Contact with Europe changed the lives and history of the groups of people living in the regions that make up modern Nigeria. The first contact came in 1471 when a group of Portuguese traders on their way to India for spices landed on the western coast of Africa. These traders met the people living around the coast, bought spices and ivory, and returned home, where they spread the news of their discovery. The report that a group of people living near the coast of West Africa exchanged valuable spices and ivory for such trifles as beads and cheap liquor encouraged traders from other European countries to investigate. By the seventeenth century, the Dutch, the French, and the British were regular visitors to the coast. And what had begun as a goodwill trading in ivory and spices quickly degenerated into the slave trade, the eventual subjugation of the people under British colonialism, independence, and a civil war.

THE SLAVE TRADE

The Europeans' arrival in the Americas and the establishment of the Spanish colonies in the West Indies created a demand for workers to cultivate the land. Neither the migrating Europeans nor the Native Americans conscripted to work the land could meet that demand. Many suggested that perhaps Africans could be brought to the new world to provide the much-needed labor. European nations, lacking in agricultural workers themselves, also looked to Africa to obtain the labor force needed to sustain their agriculturally based economies. None of the people who conceived the idea of importing Africans to the Americas and Europe could have ever imagined the proportions their suggestion would take and the consequences for African peoples.

Over the next three hundred years, about 60 million Africans would be sold into slavery and transported to Western Europe and the Americas. It is estimated that about half of them came from what is now Nigeria. At the port of Bonny alone, in the modern delta region, about twenty thousand

Nigerians were sold into slavery annually during the last twenty-five years of the eighteenth century. Some of the slaves were prisoners of war; others were criminals whose punishment was to be sold as slaves. Some had innocently given themselves or their children up in order to redeem a debt, and others were victims of the various raiding and kidnapping activities that increasingly became part of daily life. The captives were chained and marched to the coast, where they were crowded into prisons until they could be sold.

At the beginning of the nineteenth century, many Christian organizations began to campaign against the slave trade. These organizations, headed by men such as William Wilber-

Nigerian slave traders march their chained captives to the prisons where they will be held until sold.

force and Thomas Clarkson, argued that slavery was cruel and cheapened human life, and therefore should be abolished. Their cause was helped by the industrial revolution, then in full swing in Europe. Industry was gradually replacing agriculture as the basis of the European economy, and the shift meant that the unskilled labor provided by slaves was no longer necessary. Machines and skilled labor were required for the new economy. The abolitionist campaign, combined with the demands of the new industry-based economy, prompted many European nations to prohibit the slave trade. Denmark prohibited slave trading in 1804, Britain in 1807. By 1814, other European countries had followed suit. British and French naval patrols were then stationed on West African waters to help stop slave trading.

However, even though slaves were no longer needed in Europe, they were still in demand in the Americas, despite the fact that the United States banned the importation of slaves in 1808. The American demand for slaves meant that slave trading was still a profitable business, and most traders found ways to avoid the naval patrols. Of every four slave ships that left the coast, only one was caught. It is estimated that more slaves were transported to the Americas after slave trading had been prohibited than in the previous centuries combined. And the slaves were treated worse than before. If a slave trader was chased by a patrol, he would commonly throw his chained slaves overboard to destroy the evidence against him. It was not until 1852 that the last slave ship left the West African coast and many of the slave ports were captured and destroyed.

THE PALM OIL TRADE

During the first half of the nineteenth century, in the years following the ban on slave trading, European traders on the coast were pressured to find another profitable business to replace the trade in slaves. The native product they found to fit the bill was palm oil, made from the fruits of the palm trees that grew in abundance in western and eastern Nigeria and around the Niger Delta. The palm fruits are boiled briefly and then pounded to separate the pulp from the kernel (nut). The pulp is then squeezed by hand to produce the oil. Palm oil is useful for cooking, and in the manufacture of soap, lotions, and other household products.

THE SLAVE TRADE

Many Nigerians were sold into slavery during the slave trade. In his book *History of Nigeria*, Alan Burns describes the inhumanity of the European slave trade.

It is difficult . . . to conceive the amount of misery caused by the slave trade during the three centuries that it flourished in West Africa, or the degrading effect it had both on the Negroes and the scarcely more civilized whites who enriched themselves at the expense of their fellow men. The numbers that suffered and died in the barracoons [temporary housing where slaves were kept until they were sold] and slave-ships formed only a part of those affected by the constant raids and the inter-tribal wars which were waged for the purpose of making slaves. The chiefs were not averse from raiding even villages belonging to their own tribes if it was necessary to obtain slaves at once for some impatient dealer. Villages were sometimes surrounded at night and set on fire, the wretched inhabitants being seized as they escaped from the flames, those useless as slaves being butchered in cold blood to satisfy the lust for cruelty. It is true that slavery has been an institution in Africa from time immemorial, and that slaves were bought and sold on the West African coast before the first European arrived here, but owing to the enormous demand caused by the establishment of plantations in the New World, and the greater facilities provided by fire-arms for the slave-raiding chiefs, the trade increased by leaps and bounds under European management.

The uses of palm oil made it a valuable commodity. The British share of the palm oil trade at the time was estimated at more than 1 million British pounds a year. Because a lot of money was at stake, the trading companies quarreled among themselves and with African traders about their share of the oil trade and about whose laws and customs should be used in judging disputes. To guard Britain's interests, British naval ships were sent to protect English traders on the coast. Eventually, British consuls were sent to the region to intervene in the commercial disputes. This became the first step toward the eventual British occupation and colonization of the entire region north and south of the Niger River.

Transition to Colonial Rule

The first British consul appointed to the region was John Beecroft, who felt that his duty was to do everything in his power to safeguard the palm oil trade. He believed that the best way to solve the disputes between the traders was to gain control over the land. If the land officially belonged to Britain, he reasoned, then British laws could be enforced in the territory. Under the pretext that he was working to stop illegal trading in slaves, Beecroft signed treaties with native chiefs for jurisdiction over their land. Those who refused to give up control over their lands were simply deposed, and more cooperative individuals were put in their place. Other consuls after Beecroft continued the practice. By the 1870s, the British government, through its consuls, had acquired the land around the coast and were making plans to gain control over the rest of the land north and south of the Niger.

A conference held in Berlin, Germany, in 1884 aided the British quest to bring the Niger area under its control. Rival European countries organized this conference to decide which of them would colonize various parts of Africa. Since

Palm oil, derived from palm oil trees (shown), became a profitable business for the British following the ban on slave trading.

Britain had already obtained some of the land around the Niger by signing treaties with native chiefs, it was given possession of the whole Niger region. Following the conference, Britain increased its campaign to bring the areas south and north of the Niger under its control. Troops were sent into the areas, and their commanders were ordered to make treaties with village chiefs or leaders and to overthrow those who refused to sign over their lands. By 1893, the British controlled the region south of the Niger and referred to it as the Southern Protectorate. The British gained complete control of the northern region, known as the Northern Protectorate, in 1914. Later that same year, the Northern and Southern Protectorates were united to form one country. Lord Frederick Lugard, the consul-general in the region, was appointed its governor-general. The country was named Nigeria, after the Niger River.

THE BRITISH RULE

Even though the British had gained control over the various regions that made up Nigeria, governing the country posed a challenge because there was no uniform system of government among the various ethnic groups. Ultimately, the British came up with a system known as indirect rule. Instead of ruling the natives directly, the British officers ruled them through their own leaders or people appointed as leaders. In the north among the Hausas and the Fulanis, the British ruled through the emirs; in the southwest among the Yorubas, they ruled through the *obas*. Among the Ibos in the southeast, warrant chiefs were appointed to rule the people.

A chain of command was created to ensure that the system worked. An emir, an *oba*, or a warrant chief was in charge of a town or village. His duty was to protect British commercial activities in his village or town and to collect taxes. Villages and towns were grouped into several districts under the supervision of a British colonial officer called a resident. Each resident then reported to the governor-general.

Even though indirect rule was created to protect existing political institutions, it created more problems than it solved, mostly because the British were ignorant of the nuances in the natives' political structures. In the north, where a system of checks and balances had helped prevent abuses by the emirs and his officials, the British gave the emir ab-

BRITISH ECONOMIC LEGACY

In his essay in *Nigeria: A Country Study*, E. Wayne Nafziger discusses the British economic activities in Nigeria during the colonial period.

> The European construction of forts and trading posts on the West African coast from the mid-1600s to the mid-1700s was part of the wider competition for trade and empire in the Atlantic. The British, like other newcomers to the slave trade, found they could compete with the Dutch in West Africa only by forming national trading companies [a trading company under the protection of a nation]. The first such effective English enterprise was the Company of the Royal Adventurers, chartered in 1660 and succeeded in 1672 by the Royal African Company. Only a monopoly company [a company in sole control of all the trading activities in its area] could afford to build and maintain the forts considered essential to hold stocks of slaves and trade goods. In the early eighteenth century, Britain and France destroyed the Dutch hold on the West African trade; and by the end of the French Revolution and subsequent Napoleonic Wars (1799–1815), Britain had become the dominant commercial power in West Africa.

solute authority, which he had never had before. Instead of being accountable to the people, the emir was now accountable to the British resident. Among the Yorubas, where the *oba* had been only a nominal ruler and true power had rested with the council of chiefs, the British invested power in the *oba*, and thus upset the traditional government. The *oba* was given absolute authority free from traditional restraints. Not surprisingly, the natives did not particularly approve of this new system of government being imposed on them.

The Ibos, who had never had centralized government, fared even worse than the Yorubas under indirect rule. The British condemned the egalitarian nature of the Ibo political institutions, calling it primitive. They installed rulers known as warrant chiefs in place of community leadership in which everyone had a say in the administration of the village. The warrant chiefs were given absolute authority over the people and, more often than not, were chosen from low elements in society, especially since community elders refused to participate in the new colonial government. So not only were chiefs imposed on the Ibos for the first time in their history, but they came from a class the people would not ordinarily listen to. Therefore, the Ibos despised the warrant chiefs and failed to recognize them as real rulers. The incompatibility between British rule and the people's way of life set the stage for the people's revolt against imperialism and their demand for independence.

NATIONALISM AND INDEPENDENCE

The decades following the creation of Nigeria and the introduction of indirect rule saw many organized revolts against the colonial government. One famous revolt is the Aba Women's Riot of 1929, in which a small group of women protesting the intrusion of colonial activities into their lives galvanized thousands of other women into a revolt that lasted for months. World War II also contributed to the spirit of revolt and the spread of nationalism in Nigeria. During the war, many Nigerians were recruited to fight on the side of Britain. The soldiers met people from other parts of Africa and the world. They heard about the fight for freedom in other African countries under colonial regimes and about the democratic system of government practiced in Europe. When the soldiers came back, they spread the news of nationalism and self-government and fueled the people's demand for independence. Organized rallies demanding that the British "go home" became frequent.

By the late 1940s, it was obvious to British officials in Nigeria that their control of the country would not last much longer. At home, in the aftermath of World War II, Britons increasingly favored giving the British colonies in both Asia and Africa their independence. As a result, colonial officers in Nigeria worked through the 1950s to prepare Nigerians for self-government. Indirect rule was abandoned in favor of a more democratic and centralized system. The position of traditional rulers and leaders became chiefly ceremonial, as real political power was vested in the centralized government. The country was divided into three regions—the north, the west, and the east, with Lagos as its capital. The regions corresponded to the traditional lands of the three largest ethnic groups in the country—the Hausas in the north, the Yorubas in the west, and the Ibos in the east. Each region was to be self-governing in internal matters but recognize the authority of the central government in Lagos to deal with matters affecting the whole country.

Nigeria achieved independence on October 1, 1960. The makeup of the central government was intended to share power among the three major ethnic groups. The prime minister, Sir Tafawa Balewa, was a Hausa; the president, whose position was chiefly ceremonial, was Nnamdi Azikiwe, an Ibo. Obafemi Awolowo, a Yoruba, was the leader of the national assembly. Even though the new administration was constructed to reflect political unity, it belied the fact that the country that the British handed over to Nigerians was at best divided socially and politically.

AFTER INDEPENDENCE

Although the Hausas, the Yorubas, and the Ibos had agreed to join together to form an independent nation, it was not without fears or hesitation. These groups of people had not had much contact before the British came and had continued to lead separate lives during colonial rule. They each feared political domination by the others, and the tension led to many frictions and occasional violent clashes among the groups. The first task of the new administration was to find a way to unify the people.

Unfortunately, the new administration proved unable to meet the needs of the country. Corruption and internal divisions plagued and weakened both regional and federal governments. The public grew increasingly disillusioned about their new leaders' abilities to meet their needs. There was a growing sentiment that perhaps the military would provide better leadership for the country and bring peace and unity.

The sentiment became a reality in January 1966 when the military overthrew the government in a violent coup. Most of the country's political leaders were assassinated, including the prime minister. The military leaders pledged to establish a strong and efficient government that would bring unity.

Prime Minister Sir Tafawa Balewa, a Hausa, was the first prime minister in Nigeria after it gained independence from Britain on October 1, 1960.

They vowed to stamp out corruption and to hold new elections in the near future.

The only problem was that the coup had been organized and carried out primarily by Ibo military officers from the east, and most of the assassinated leaders were from the northern and western regions. Therefore, rather than providing unity, the coup only aggravated existing ethnic fears. As one writer notes, "The coup was perceived not so much as an effort to impose a unitary government [but] as a plot by the Ibos to dominate Nigeria."[3] Violence between the ethnic groups, especially the Ibos and the Hausas, increased. The Hausas opposed the new government, while the Ibos fa-

THE FIRST COUP

Nigeria experienced the first military overthrow of a civilian government in 1966. Even though Nigerians initially welcomed the coup, it later sowed the seeds of distrust that led to the Nigerian civil war. In his essay "Politics Since Independence," published in the book *Nigerian History and Culture*, Leo Dare discusses the circumstances.

By the time the military intervened in January 1966, it had become obvious to all observers that the civilian regime had failed in its primary function of maintaining law and order. The masses became desperate in their quest for an effective government. It was mainly because of dissatisfaction with the civilian administration and because the military appeared to give them hope of a better government that the military coup of 15 January 1966 was hailed so widely. It was a popular operation. . . . The coup leader demonstrated this awareness of public despair when in its first broadcast he stated that the coup was designed to "bring an end to gangsterism and disorder, corruption and despotism" and ended by saying "my compatriots, you will no longer be ashamed to be Nigerians."

Within three days of the initial announcement of the coup, it had become clear that . . . the victims of the coup were predominantly non-Ibo while the planners were Ibo. Due to this, a cloud of suspicion later hung over the coup and its successor regime. . . . Even with the best of goodwill, Ironsi [the military head of state] would have to prove that his regime had not come about to preserve Ibo interests.

vored it. Within a year, the violent clashes had grown into a civil war, known as the Nigerian-Biafran War.

Soldiers from the Biafran National Army fought for independence from Nigeria's Hausa-led government in 1970.

THE CIVIL WAR

Amid feelings that the coup was nothing but an attempt by the Ibos to control the rest of the country, fighting broke out between Hausa and Ibo soldiers stationed in the southeast. In June, mobs in the northern cities, encouraged by local officials, massacred hundreds of Ibo residents and destroyed Ibo-owned properties. Those who survived the massacre fled home to the south, demanding revenge against the Hausas.

In July, barely six months after the Ibo-led coup, Hausa officers staged a countercoup, in which the head of the new government, Aguiyi Ironsi, and many other Ibo officers were killed. Lieutenant Colonel (later Major General) Yakubu Gowon was named the head of state. Gowon's government tried to restore order, but the violence increased. By September, as many

PEACE

At the end of the Nigerian civil war, many Ibos were concerned that the federal government would mistreat them because they had lost the war. But the head of state, General Gowon, promised to grant amnesty to the Ibos and reintegrate them into Nigerian social and political life. Even though many Ibos doubted his sincerity, he kept his word. The following, quoted by Jean Herskovits in the book *Nigeria: Power and Democracy in Africa*, is a speech Gowon broadcast to the nation on January 15, 1970, the day the Ibos surrendered their quest to secede.

> I solemnly repeated our guarantees of general amnesty for those misled into rebellion. We guarantee the personal safety of everyone who submits to the federal authority. We guarantee the security of life and property of all citizens in every part of Nigeria, and equality in political rights. We also guarantee the right of every Nigerian to reside and work wherever he chooses in the federation as equal citizens of one united country. It is only right that we should all henceforth respect each other. We should all exercise civic restraint and use our freedom taking into account the legitimate rights and needs of the other man. There is no question of second-class citizenship in Nigeria.

as thirty thousand Ibos living in the northern cities had been killed. Hausas living in the east were massacred in response.

In this atmosphere of ethnic division and violence, the Ibo military governor, Lieutenant Colonel Chukuwemeka Odumegwu Ojukwu, announced in May 1967 that the Ibos would secede from Nigeria and form their own country under the name the Independent Republic of Biafra. He accused the federal government of genocide and indicated that the decision to secede was being made reluctantly but that it was necessary to safeguard the lives of the Ibo people.

The federal government of Nigeria did not want the Ibos to leave the union. Therefore, it refused to recognize Biafra's independence. The government officials and Ibo leaders met to find a compromise. But when negotiations failed, federal troops were sent into the Ibo region to quell the rebellion and force the Ibos back into the union. They were met with stubborn resistance by the Ibo soldiers. The war lasted for three years, with fierce fighting on each side. But the federal soldiers were better equipped and finally broke down Ibo resistance.

On January 6, 1970, Ojukwu fled to the Ivory Coast when Ibo resistance collapsed. His chief of staff, Philip Effiong, called for an immediate cease-fire and surrendered unconditionally to the authority of the federal government in Lagos. In all, an estimated 1 to 3 million Ibos had lost their lives during the war, and property damage was estimated at 600 billion naira (about $900 billion). Many villages, towns, and cities in Iboland had been destroyed.

The Ibos worried that they would be made to live in disgrace because they had lost the war. But General Gowon, in a remarkable spirit of peace and unity, declared that there would be no victor and no vanquished. They were simply all

In the period following the civil war, General Gowon rebuilt Nigeria's infrastructure and normalized relationships with other countries that supported the Biafran revolt.

The three-year Nigerian civil war brought human misery and deprivation to the country's citizens, many of whom were on the brink of starvation at war's end.

Nigerians. In the years that followed the war, efforts were made in the spirit of Gowon's statement to reintegrate the Ibos into the political life of the country and to rebuild the infrastructures that had been damaged during the war. Gowon also normalized Nigeria's relationship with all the countries that had supported the Biafran quest for independence.

The Ibos today are fully integrated into Nigerian life, but the problems that led to the civil war have not yet been solved. The nation still faces the challenges of accommodating the demands and fears of its diverse ethnic groups. Nigeria's political life and calculations center on achieving a balance of power among its various peoples. The formula for unity has remained elusive.

Nigerian Government and Politics

In the early 1980s, a popular Nigerian musician, Sonny Okosun, released a record titled "Which Way Nigeria?" The song became very popular because it asked the question on the minds of most Nigerians: Where were the political affairs of their country headed? Two decades later, Nigerians are still seeking the answer to that question. The difficulty comes from the fact that the nation has faced—and continues to face—many challenges. The country has suffered from many years of ineffective and corrupt leadership, especially at the hands of its military, and from ethnic and religious conflicts. These problems have weakened both the political and economic systems and have demoralized the people. Nigeria must find a way to meet its political and economic challenges in order to achieve stability and prosperity.

A Troubled Military Heritage

The history of postindependence Nigeria has to a large extent been intertwined with the history of the military. Unlike in many Western countries where there is a separation between the military and politics, the Nigerian military has always been involved in the nation's politics. Most Nigerians think that the military sees itself as another branch of government, that it has assigned itself the double roles of defending as well as ruling the country.

Since the first military overthrow of the government in 1966, the military has viewed itself as the political savior of the country. Whenever the country is faced with the inefficiency of its elected leaders, the military has felt compelled to intervene. Nigeria has been under seven military administrations since independence and has experienced many more failed coups. However, instead of solving the country's problems and moving it forward, the military has complicated things further. Military leaders are not trained to rule. Therefore, many of them have no skill or thought-out plan on how to govern the nation. They have also not been above corruption. Most of the military men who have ruled Nigeria have been unwilling to give up power voluntarily. Many have also used their position to embezzle the nation's money. They send public funds to foreign private bank accounts, stealing from the people when most of the people are having difficulty making ends meet.

"COUP FROM HEAVEN"

Nigeria's most recent period of military rule began with a coup in 1992 when Major General Sani Abacha organized a bloodless overthrow of the government and made himself the president. He was a dictator who jailed, without trial, many people who opposed his rule. His regime lasted until June 1998, when he died of a sudden heart attack. Many Nigerians consider his death a "coup from heaven," referring to the belief that nothing short of death would have removed him from the head of Nigerian government.

Abacha's second in command, General Abdulsalami-Abubakar, took office and did something quite remarkable

A "WORKSHOP OF DEMOCRACY"

Since independence from Britain, Nigeria has had both civilian and military administrations. However, as Eghosa Osaghae discusses in an essay published in *Nigeria: A Country Study*, the structure of the country's different administrations has been quite similar.

If any nation typifies political scientist Richard Sklar's characterization of the African continent as a "workshop of democracy," it would certainly be Nigeria. The country has experimented with different federal, state, and local government systems, learning more about its needs, resources, and constraints with each experiment. Despite the predominance of military regimes during the three post-colonial decades, Nigerian society has retained many of the fundamental building blocks of a democratic polity: vigorous entrepreneurial classes, a broad intelligentsia and numerous centers of higher education, a dynamic legal community and judiciary, diverse and often outspoken media, and increasingly, courageous human rights organizations.

for a Nigerian military man. He said that he had no interest in ruling the country and immediately made plans to return the government to civilian control. Under his leadership, elections were held, and the nation chose Olusegun Obasanjo, himself a former military ruler and a political prisoner under Abacha's regime, as the new head of state.

Obasanjo has pledged to work on establishing the people's confidence in their government. He flushed the military of its politically ambitious senior officers and set up investigations into corruption and human rights abuses. He describes himself as a new breed of politician, aimed at holding the country together and leading it into economic growth and prosperity. But Obasanjo's commitment has not been enough to bring about effective democracy at all levels of government. The country still needs to deal with the challenges posed by ethnic and religious conflicts, the legacy of past ineffective government structures, and a struggling economy.

Nigerian leader Olusegun Obasanjo waves to the crowd during a parade to commemorate the nation's forty years of independence.

Muslim men pray in a small mosque in Ibadan, Nigeria. The Christian and Islamic religions have equal followings throughout Nigeria.

RELIGIOUS CONFLICTS

One of the major challenges facing Nigeria is how to minimize conflicts among different religious groups. Forty-five percent of the people are Christians, 45 percent are Muslims, and 10 percent are traditional adherents. This would not be significant, except that the different religious histories of the north and the south have concentrated the majority of the Muslims in the north and the majority of the Christians in the south. Tension between the values of the Muslim north and the Christian south has been one of the defining aspects of Nigerian politics.

While the south advocates a secular system of government that is neutral to religious faith, the more militant Muslims in the north would like to see the whole country governed in accordance with Islamic principles and laws. Islamic laws, or Shari'a, require complete segregation of men and women in all aspects of life. They also prescribe stiff penalties for criminal behavior, such as cutting off the hand of a persistent thief, flogging for vandalism, and flogging or death for adultery. Muslims think that the strict application of Islamic laws would be the solution to the corruption and crimes that have always threatened the welfare of the nation. Christians, however, argue that it would be unfair to impose upon them laws from a religion they do not practice. Moreover, they point out that punishments such as amputation or death for adultery are human rights violations.

The inability of the two sides to reach a compromise has been a source of tension in the country. Deadly riots and violent clashes have been frequent. In February 2000, Christians fought with Muslims over the planned imposition of Islamic laws in the city of Kaduna. Many people on both sides were killed, and churches and mosques were destroyed. There have also been riots and clashes in other states and cities that have proposed establishing Shari'a laws. An editorial published in *Christianity Today* estimates that in 2000, more than one thousand people lost their lives during religious clashes and that the riots caused property damage amounting to billions of dollars. There are no easy solutions to these problems.

ETHNIC RIVALRIES

Religious conflicts are intensified by ethnic rivalries. Nigeria has three major ethnic groups and more than four hundred minority groups. Since independence, the major ethnic groups, the Ibos, the Hausas, and Yorubas, have distrusted and feared each other. Each feels that, if given the opportunity, the other will dominate the central government and work against the interest of other ethnic groups. This atmosphere of distrust has created a power struggle among the three dominant ethnic groups. Intended to help minimize the tension, the constitution demands that, on the national level, power must be shared equally among the groups. For example, if the president is of the Yoruba ethnic group, the vice president must be from another ethnic group, and the president of the Senate must be from the third ethnic group.

CONFLICT OVER SHARI'A LAWS

Since the return to civilian rule in 1999, Christians and Muslims have clashed over the proposed institution of Shari'a laws (Islamic laws) in some northern states. An editorial in the October 23, 2000, issue of *Christianity Today* titled "Will Shari'a Law Curb Christianity?" summarizes some of the bases of the conflict.

> The clashes between Christians and Muslims broke out in the town of Kaltunga and spread to the towns of Billiri and Bambam within two days. Tensions ran high after the Gombe government decided . . . to establish Shari'a, the Islamic legal code, as its official legal framework. Christian leaders had warned the Gombe state government that they would refuse to accept the Islamic legal system. More than 75 percent of the state's 2.7 million people are Christians. Christians maintain that the introduction of Shari'a will make it impossible for them to practice their religion. They believe Islamic law would prevent the teaching of Christianity in public schools; prevent Christians from building new churches and enable Muslims to force relocation of existing churches; discriminate against Christians in public service, since Shari'a forbids non-Muslims for having authority over Muslims; categorize single mothers as prostitutes; prevent women from traveling in the same vehicles as their husbands, even to attend church; and introduce draconian penalties, such as cutting off a thief's hand and death by stoning for those convicted of adultery. . . . The federal government, whose principal officers are divided along religious lines, seems unable to find a solution to the violence in northern Nigeria. Nigerian . . . churches are challenging in court the Islamic legal system.

In addition to the political tension among the major ethnic groups, there is also the minority issue. The other four hundred plus ethnic groups also want to be represented adequately on both the federal and state levels and have their needs met. The country has tried to solve this problem through the creation of more states. At independence, there were only three states, representing the three major ethnic groups. This meant that the major ethnic groups dominated and overshadowed the numerous minority ones. The minority groups believed that more states needed to be created to dilute the power of the major ethnic groups and give the minorities recognition and better representation. Today, there are thirty-five states and the Federal Capital Territory.

The creation of more states has minimized the resentment of the minority groups, but it has not been enough to ease conflicts completely. Some ethnic groups have as few as five hundred people. It is difficult to create a state with only five hundred people. The country has to find a way to integrate the ethnic groups and ensure that everybody has a say in the affairs of the country. This, however, will be difficult to accomplish until the different levels of government—the executive, the legislative, and the judiciary—effectively carry out their duties.

THE CIVIL SERVICE

The ineffectiveness of the Nigerian government is epitomized by the civil service, the part of the executive branch closest to the people. Modeled after the British civil service, it was created during colonial rule as the administration

These Yoruba women belong to one of the three major ethnic groups within Nigeria.

expanded to include educated natives in running the country. Natives filled needed positions, ranging from clerk to ministerial head, and since independence the service has remained a constant in the lives of the people.

The civil service includes all those serving in various capacities in the federal and state ministerial offices. This is where decisions are made and public policy initiated with the approval of the state governor or the president. Each ministerial office is headed by a member of the governor's cabinet on the state level or the president's cabinet on the

180 LASHES

Shari'a laws, opposed by Nigerian Christian groups, advocate severe penalties for people who violate Islamic laws. Punishments include cutting off the hand of a thief and flogging or stoning to death a person convicted of adultery. In 2000, an unmarried, sixteen-year-old-girl who became pregnant was tried and sentenced to be given 180 lashes for having premarital sex, considered a crime by Muslims. An editorial in the January 4, 2001, issue of the *Christian Science Monitor,*" explains the case.

> The unmarried girl, Bariya Ibrahim Magazu, was sentenced in September [2000] by an Islamic court in Tsafe in Zamfara state to be lashed 180 times after she was discovered to be pregnant. Asked who the father was, the girl named three middle-aged men from her village who she said had pressured her into engaging in sex. The judge of the local Islamic court, Idris Usman Gusau, ruled that under the terms of Islamic law introduced in Zamfara last year, she had not proven her claims against the three men. He sentenced her to 80 lashes for premarital sex and 100 for making unproven claims against the men. The lashes will be administered by police or Islamic vigilante members some 40 days after the birth of her daughter. . . . Several human rights groups, including Amnesty International . . . have expressed concern. But in an interview with journalists . . . President Olusegun Obasanjo, a Christian, said he will not intervene. Mr. Obasanjo has been criticized by many Christian leaders who see him as overcautious in his reaction to Islamic punishments being introduced by leaders of the Muslim north.

federal level. The minister then appoints a departmental secretary to help in administering the office.

The duty of the civil service is to provide social services for the people. But the civil service is notorious for its ineffectiveness and bureaucratic red tape. Most of the senior personnel are appointed because of political affiliations, and consequently feel no responsibility for the people they are supposed to serve. As one Nigerian puts it, to get something accomplished through any of the offices, "one has to know somebody who knows somebody or is prepared to pay a large sum of money in the form of a bribe to somebody."[4] The service has been undergoing restructuring to make it more responsive to the needs of the people, but as with all aspects of Nigerian politics, the problems have continued.

A STRUGGLING LEGISLATIVE BRANCH

If the civil service is crippled by red tape and indifferent workers, the legislative branch is plagued by incompetence. The structure of the legislative branch and its duties are clear. On the federal level, the legislative branch consists of the Senate, known as the National Assembly, and the House of Representatives. Members of both the Assembly and the House are elected by popular vote to serve seven-year terms. There are no term limits.

The duty of the legislative branch is to consider and make laws to be interpreted and enforced by the judiciary. However, after the 1999 elections, neither the Senate nor the House passed any laws to benefit the people. Rather, internal political squabbles were escalated by accusations of corruption. In less than two years, the national Senate impeached its president three times, the House impeached its president twice; and many members have been investigated and convicted of corruption. State legislatures have not fared better. They mirror the incompetence and corruption of the national legislature.

Most people explain the weakness of the legislative branch as a part of the legacy of military rule. Nigeria has been under military rule for thirty of its forty years since independence, so the country's legislature is still in its infancy. Its functions were always suspended during military regimes when governmental control became the sole responsibility of the military head of state and his ruling council. As a result,

THE FEDERAL GOVERNMENT

Nigeria's executive branch is made up of the president, vice president, and members of his cabinet. The president is elected by popular vote for no more than two four-year terms. He is the head of state and the commander-in-chief of the armed forces.

Like any other democratically elected ruler, the president's duty is to represent the interest of the people who elected him, to raise the people's standard of living by initiating and supporting policies that effectively tap the country's resources. Each of the president's cabinet members oversees a ministry and has the duty to keep the president informed of any developments of national or international magnitude. Members of the cabinet show the ethnic diversity of the nation. Conscious effort is made to include people from all major ethnic and minority groups in the administration.

the Nigerian legislative branch has had few precedents and no clear understanding of its duties. Its challenge, therefore, lies in the elected officials rising above self-interest, learning the rules of the offices they occupy, and focusing on carrying out the nation's business. It is obvious that the country cannot move forward with a legislative branch that does not serve the people.

A TROUBLED JUDICIARY

Although comparatively more effective than the legislative branch, the judicial system faces its own challenges. Nigeria has always had a complex legal system that is influenced by British as well as traditional laws. When Britain granted independence to Nigeria in 1960, the legal system was set up to recognize the different aspects of British laws with which the British colonial officers were most familiar and to recognize customary laws that addressed issues not covered by British laws. As with the legislative branch, the structure and duties of the judiciary are clear and consistent.

On the national level, there is the Supreme Court (the country's highest court of appeal), the federal court of appeals, and the high courts. On the state level, each has a supreme court, located in the state capital; magistrate courts; district courts; and customary courts. Cases concerning traditional customs such as inheritance, land use, and marriage are decided by the customary courts.

The president appoints federal judges and magistrates, and the governors appoint state ones. The revenue for running the court system also comes from the president or governor. This setup binds the judiciary to the executive branch and compromises the courts. Judges and magistrates are vulnerable to intimidation and corruption and often feel forced to uphold the interest of whoever appoints them. The Nigerian Association of Judges and Lawyers has asked that the judiciary be made independent of the executive branch to enable it to serve its functions adequately. Judges found to take bribes are being dismissed and prosecuted. But it will take time before the judiciary is completely rehabilitated.

A STRUGGLING ECONOMY

Although Nigeria is conscientiously working to remedy its political environment for the better, there is no question that the enormity of its past and present political problems have had a tremendously destabilizing effect on the economy. Given the size of the Nigerian population and its immense mineral and land resources, there is no reason the country's economy should not be thriving. But, with per capita income at $300, Nigeria ranks thirteenth among the poorest nations in the world.

Nigeria has not always been poor. In the 1970s, it was ranked as one of the richest nations in the world. At that

THE STATE GOVERNMENTS

In the year 2000, Nigeria had thirty-five states, thirty-two more than the three it had at its independence in 1960. The country sees the creation of many states as a way to dilute the power of the major ethnic groups and offer minority groups a responsible state government that represents and meets the needs of its people. The structure of the state government parallels that of the federal government in that it has three branches of government—the executive, headed by the governor and members of his cabinet; the legislature; and the judiciary. The state government is responsible for structural and economic development of its area; it also provides its people social services such as health and education.

time, the Nigerian economy was based on agriculture and manufacturing. Farmers produced enough food for the country and had enough left over to be exported to other countries. Nigeria was a major exporter of cocoa, peanuts, rubber, corn, and palm products. It was also the biggest poultry producer in Africa, with an output of 40 million birds annually. This all changed with the oil boom of the 1970s and the subsequent mismanagement of the economy by corrupt and ineffective leaders.

Oil pipelines are laid in the Niger Delta, where the promise of wealth in the oil industry has lured farmers from agricultural work.

Oil was discovered on the southern shores of Nigeria during the late 1950s. By 1970, Nigeria was experiencing an oil boom. Initially, the income from oil helped build new infrastructures and update existing ones. The economy seemed to be on the right course. But, over time, the large revenue coming from the oil, and the lack of foresight and planning by the military government, led the country to neglect its strong agricultural and manufacturing industries in favor of dependence on oil.

THE SHIFT TO OIL

Many young people seeking a share of the oil money abandoned the rural areas and farmlands for the cities. Farming was then mostly carried on by women, old men, and children left behind in the rural areas. The consequences of the shift from agriculture to oil were enormous for the country. First, the few farmers in the rural areas were unable to produce enough food. Food became scarce, and Nigeria went from being a major exporter of food to having to import food to feed its people. Second, although the production of cash crops such as cocoa and peanuts continued, the output became low and profit very marginal. Third, many of the young people who arrived in the cities from the rural areas found that there were not enough jobs to go around. Even though some industries managed to remain in operation, many shut down because of insufficient raw materials from the rural areas. Poverty became a fact of life as the prices of goods skyrocketed. Since 1970, Nigeria's annual inflation rate has remained at 15 percent.

In the 1980s and '90s, haphazard effort was made to redirect the people's attention to agriculture. Most of the effort failed because of corruption. Leaders borrowed money from the world bank to loan to farmers at low interest rates and to purchase modern farm equipment. But they either embezzled the money or loaned it to people who did not use it on the farms or repay the loans. And government officials frequently lacked the moral courage to prosecute and punish those who misused the loans because they too were corrupt. Nigeria's foreign debt is about $30 billion, and about 75 percent of it was embezzled or mismanaged.

Falling oil prices in the 1990s did not help the Nigerian economy. Low revenues resulted in the government not having enough money to run the country. Even though oil prices have subsequently risen, the current quota-based production enforced by the Organization of Petroleum Exporting Countries (OPEC) has ensured lower revenues. Therefore, the government has continued to be unable to meet the people's needs. Basic infrastructures like oil refineries, roads, and power plants are in disrepair. The irony is that, although Nigeria is an oil-producing country, its inadequate local refineries prevent it from meeting its internal oil needs. As a result, gasoline in Nigeria is very expensive and there are constantly long lines at gas stations. Even waiting in line for hours at a gas station is not a guarantee that one will get gasoline. This is only one way the state of the economy makes the people's lives difficult.

The current democratically elected Nigerian administration says that Nigeria has learned its lessons. Citing a lack of accountability and corruption as the roots of the country's problem, the administration has vowed to stamp out cor-

Nigeria's government attempted to revitalize the country's agricultural market, though without much success, when food and raw materials became scarce commodities.

REFORM

Since coming into office in 1999, Nigerian president Olusegun Obasanjo has pledged to help the country recover from years of economic abuse and to take measures to foster prosperity. The task has not been easy, as an editorial in the December 16, 2000, issue of the *Economist* indicates.

Nigeria is Africa's most populous country and home to some of its poorest people. But it also earned $280 billion from oil sales over the past 30 years, money that vanished during the years of corruption and mismanagement under military rule. Mr. Obasanjo, who was once a military ruler himself but was elected president last year as a civilian, claims that his government is more open and more committed to reform than that of any of his predecessors. . . . But [economic] progress . . . has been slower than many would have liked. Despite the rise in the world price of oil, Mr. Obasanjo [argues] that Nigeria could not meet the repayments on its debt that amounts to more than 75% of GDP [its gross domestic product]. It was a choice, he implied, of repaying the debt or building roads, schools and health clinics. On the other hand, debt relief would allow him to give the long-suffering Nigerian public a "democracy dividend," a sign that something is at last going right now that military rule has come to an end.

ruption and revive the economy. Internal checks and balances have been instituted to oversee contract awards and to make sure that projects are completed on time. Plans are being made to update and repair Nigerian infrastructures. There are also plans to diversify the economy so that the country is no longer reliant solely on oil. But all these will take time. If it took the military thirty years of nonpolicy to destroy a once-vibrant economy, it will take a civilian administration, however effective, more than a year or two to repair the damage.

5

EVERYDAY LIFE

Life in Nigeria is a combination of traditional ways of life and ways of life that are emerging as a result of contact with the outside world. Nigerians, no matter where they live, feel the influence of both. However, there is a sharp contrast between life in the rural areas and life in the cities. Village life maintains many aspects of traditional living; life in the urban centers, while retaining indigenous flavor, moves gradually toward newer cultural attitudes.

LIFE IN THE RURAL AREAS

Although Nigeria has many cities and towns, an estimated 67 percent of its population lives in rural areas. Life in these areas retains its precolonial, traditional flavor, but changes are also apparent. There are many ranch-style and two-story houses as well as mud or adobe brick houses with aluminum or thatched roofs. The mud houses are usually very few because families build cement brick houses as soon as they can afford it. Mud houses are viewed as an indicator of extremely low social status and poverty.

Life in the villages is organized around the extended family, all of whom live together in large family compounds or at least live near each other. A compound can contain anywhere from two to ten houses to accommodate the number of people who live in it. For the most part, those who live in the rural areas are the elderly, women whose husbands have left the villages to find better economic opportunities in the cities, and their children. Once gainfully employed, the men usually send money back to their families on a regular basis. But, despite these funds, most people in the villages still have to farm to make ends meet. This is why, except in the north where women's activities are limited because of Islamic laws, the majority of Nigerian farmers today are women. They work on family lands, producing crops that are taken to the cities to be sold. The profit is then used to buy what the family can't produce on its own.

Health and social services are poor in the rural communities. There are community health centers and maternity homes, but

most are ill equipped and understaffed. The very sick often have to travel to the nearest city to get help. Many people, as a result, rely on native medicine to cure most illness.

Electricity and running water are often lacking in the villages. Those who can afford it—and few can—use generators to produce light and have individual water tanks or water holes. Others use candles and kerosene lamps for light. Water is obtained from streams or springs, some of which are at least six miles from the villages. Some villages have central pumps that are turned on twice a day, in the morning and in the evening. Children often line up in front of the pumps and take turns filling buckets or other containers. The children balance these containers on their heads to carry them home, where the water is used for cooking and drinking. Cooking takes place over open wood stoves; few people have access to gas or kerosene stoves. Electric stoves are virtually nonexistent.

Recently, some communities have organized self-help groups with the aim of improving the local standard of living.

Nigerians in rural areas develop their social lives around the extended family.

A man sits in front of his farmhouse made of thatched grass and mud in Toro, Nigeria.

Members contribute money to bring electricity and pipeborne water into the villages. The problem is that individual families still have to tap into the water supply and electric lines to bring these necessities into their houses, and not many families can afford to do so.

In spite of the low standard of living in the villages, village life is vibrant, and for the most part, it forms the core of existence for many Nigerians. The lack of electricity does not impede activities because the villagers have learned to adjust their lives to what is available. Stores are open well into the night hours with the help of kerosene lamps; relatives visit each other after chores are done; and nighttime family gatherings are a way of life. The practice of land tenure also means that family lands remain within the family, and no matter where one goes to make a living within or outside Nigeria, home is still in the villages. Many people return to the villages upon retirement, and the village is where great occasions like weddings and births are celebrated. When a person dies, the body is transported back to the village to be buried among ancestors. During holidays, Christmas and Easter in particular, most who live in the cities return to the villages to rest and celebrate. No matter how urbanized Nigeria becomes, the villages will remain a central part of the people's lives.

LIFE IN THE CITIES

The harsh daily existence of rural life means that many people, especially the younger ones, migrate to urban centers annually in search of an improved standard of living. Today, because of urban migration, Nigeria has some of the most

LAGOS

Until 1990, Lagos was the capital of Nigeria. In that year, the capital was moved to Abuja on the grounds that Abuja had a more centralized location and that Lago's location on the coast made it easily accessible to enemy attack or invasion. But, as John Owhonda states in his book *Nigeria: A Nation of Many Peoples*, no other Nigerian city compares to Lagos.

The Lagos metropolitan area has more than 12 million inhabitants living in its city proper, its manicured suburbs, and its busy shantytowns. Like New York City, Lagos has many high-rise buildings and bridges that span its waterways, connecting its many islands. This former capital of Nigeria is a noisy city that is full of activity. . . . Before the Portuguese gave the city its present name, Lagos was known as Eko and was a small fishing port. Today it is the leading commercial and manufacturing center in Nigeria. The National Museum, National Theater, and Tafawa Balewa Square are only a few of the city's attractions. The city takes pride in its mixture of Brazilian, European, and African architecture. The vibrant lifestyle of its citizens, its nightclubs, bustling ports, and blend of African and Western cultures make Lagos an exciting place to live and visit.

rapidly growing cities in Africa. Each of the thirty-five state capitals has more than 100,000 inhabitants. Lagos, considered the most vibrant city in West Africa, boasts a population of 12 million; Ibadan has 5 million; Kano, 1 million; and Enugu, 500,000. The population in all of these cities virtually doubles every fifteen years. These cities, along with the hundreds of smaller towns of more than twenty thousand inhabitants, suggest that the extent of Nigeria's urbanization is probably more widespread than in anywhere else in Africa.

Nigeria has a full range of industries, all of which are concentrated in the cities and provide employment opportunities. They include food processing, motor vehicles, textiles, paper, cement, pharmaceuticals, beverages, refined petroleum, iron and steel, and shoe manufacturing. Government agencies and offices and private firms in the cities also provide places of employment. There are doctors, nurses, teachers, and lawyers that staff both public and private civil enterprises.

Boats are anchored in the bay of Lagos, Nigeria, one of Africa's fastest-growing cities.

A merchant holds up a piece of fabric he is peddling at an open market in Kano, Nigeria. Nigerians are known for their excellent salesmanship.

However, the majority of those who live in the city are businesspeople. They sell goods and provide services in well-established open markets, which form the center of urban activities. Nigerians are known as great merchants, and many have networks that extend throughout Nigeria and to other African and world countries. The main market in Onitsha is the largest of its kind in West Africa, covering a space of more than five miles. There are also warehouses, supermarkets, and convenience stores in major streets and strategic places around the city.

Life in the city begins at 6:00 in the morning, as many begin to make their way to their places of employment. Many people commute to work using taxis or minibuses. Taxis are the favorite form of public transportation in the cities, and one can hail taxis on the streets. Buses are less expensive than taxis, but they are slower and less convenient. They make frequent stops and are limited in the routes they cover. Markets open at 8:00 A.M. and close at 6:00 P.M. All sorts of things, from televisions to clothing to food items, are bought and sold in the markets. Supermarkets are open very late, some till midnight. Lunch is available in the many food stalls and canteens in the markets and restaurants scattered around the city. But stores do not close during the lunch break. Workers take their lunch breaks in shifts.

An important aspect of business practice in Nigeria is the system of apprenticeship. Apprentices work for individual employers. They may be relatives or children of family friends. They live with their business mentors for a specified amount of time, from two to seven years, helping in general aspects of business life and household duties as they learn the trade. During their years of apprenticeship, students are expected to establish business connections that will help them when they are on their own. At the end of the apprenticeship, mentors are expected to provide the students with the financial resources to start their own business. How much money a mentor invests in the student, however, depends on the mentor's discretion and generosity.

HARSHNESS OF CITY LIFE

Life in Nigerian cities involves a mix of different ethnic groups and peoples from varying walks of life. There are many forms of entertainment available, including museums, nightclubs, cinema, theater, and opera. But the city also has many disadvantages. Most young people who leave the rural areas for the promise of a better life in the cities quickly realize that life in the city can also be harsh, perhaps even more so because of the lack of family support that is readily available in the villages. One in every four Nigerians is unemployed, and most of the country's poor live in the cities. Housing in the cities is scarce, which often results in squalid living conditions for those struggling to survive.

Physically, Nigerian cities look like any other city in the developed world, with bungalows, high-rise buildings, and ghettos. The gap between the haves and the have-nots is quite obvious. Most of the poor live in crowded housing and shanties scattered all over the city, which contrast sharply with the tall office buildings and the flats and villas of the middle class and the rich.

The cities have running water and electricity, but neither is reliable. City dwellers can go for months without either. As in the rural areas, kerosene and pressure lamps and candles are used for light. Kerosene or gas stoves are popular because they do not depend on electricity. Young people spend a great deal of time in the evenings looking for water and buying it wherever they can find it. Aware that electricity and water are vital elements in the development of the economy, the government is working to increase the adequacy of NEPA (Nigerian Electric Power and Authority), the government-owned agency responsible for hydroelectricity.

THE FAMILY

In both the rural areas and the city, the family forms the basis of social life. Polygamy is permitted because Islam allows

Poor citizens living in the larger cities inhabit crowded, run-down housing areas such as this one in Lagos, Nigeria.

a man to marry up to four wives, and traditional African religion allows a man to marry as many wives as he can afford. Education and Christianity, however, have made polygamous marriages the exception rather than the rule.

Most Nigerians will agree that although tradition allows huge families, modern economic realities preclude the practice. In the past when many children were needed to help farm the land, multiple wives and children were the ideal. The family produced enough food for themselves and had surplus to sell in the markets. Today, the economy is no longer based on farming, so multiple wives and children are

Although, traditionally, Nigerian men may marry as many wives as they can afford, polygamy has become outmoded.

no longer seen as an economic necessity. As a result, the average Nigerian family consists of a husband, a wife, and their children. Women living in the cities usually have fewer children, about three or four, than those living in the rural areas. The average number of children for a Nigerian woman is six.

Children are expected to marry when they reach adulthood. Marriages are not arranged, although the family does exert great influence on the choice of a spouse. Not many men and women marry a person their families disapprove of. The groom pays a bride-price, a small token of money, for his wife. Even though most couples marry for love, Nigerians believe that the primary purpose of any marriage is to produce children. Children are valuable because they carry on the family name and provide support for aging parents. Since there are no government-administered social security programs and no nursing or retirement homes, the elderly live with members of their families, who provide for them emotionally and financially. Care and respect for the elderly is expected; they are viewed as the repositories of wisdom and traditional life.

LEISURE AND SPORTS

Knowing that many people, including parents, are dependent on their success, most Nigerians work hard to make a living. Because of this, most would say that leisure is only for the rich. However, this would be stretching the truth since people do not work all the time without resting. When daily activities are done, men and women mingle in restaurants and bars in the cities, enjoying a drink or dancing and telling stories. In the villages, after the planting season or the harvest, men and women pursue hobbies such as weaving and carving. Although some of the products are used by the family or sold, the primary emphasis is on the enjoyment of the activity and the honing of one's skills. Children occupy their free time playing games such as *mankala* and hopscotch or learning dances for social occasions.

Wrestling is a form of entertainment and leisure for many. In traditional society, community wrestling was part of every festival, and wrestlers were honored and valued as much as warriors. They represented the village's strength, and each victory was a victory for the village of the wrestler. Today, there are amateur wrestling organizations for those

PRAISE FOR A CHILD

Nigerians value children, as is depicted in this anonymous, sentimental poem from Ruth Finnegan's *A World Treasury of Oral Poetry.*

A child is like a rare bird.
A child is precious like coral.
A child is precious like brass.
You cannot buy a child on the market.
Not for all the money in the world.
The child you can buy for money is a slave.
We may have twenty slaves.
We may have thirty laborers.
Only a child brings us joy.
One's child is one's child.
The buttocks of a child are not so flat
That we should tie the beads on another child's hips.
One's child is one's child.
It may have watery head or a square head,
One's child is one's child.
It is better to leave behind a child
Than let the slaves inherit one's house.
One must not rejoice too soon over a child.
Only the one who is buried by his child
Is the one who has truly borne a child.
On the day of our death, our hand cannot hold a single
     cowrie.
We need a child to inherit our belongings.

interested in the sport. But wrestling does not have as much of a following as soccer.

Soccer is by far the most popular sport in Nigeria. Every boy dreams of growing up and one day playing like his soccer hero. There are community, state, and national teams. Players from various clubs compete for the national championship, known as the Challenge Cup. A professional soccer league was created in 1990. The national team consists of the Green Eagles and the Junior Eagles, who represent the nation in international games such as the World Cup, the Olympic Games, and the African Cup of Nations Championship. The Nigerian Eagles are familiar faces in the international soccer community. They won the gold medal during the 1996 Summer Olympic Games in Atlanta; they have also won the African Cup of Nations Championship matches many times. There is also a strong national women's soccer team who won the 1998 African Women's Soccer Championship. But women's sports have yet to enjoy the same level of popularity and support as men's sports.

Track and field is perhaps the second most popular sport. The Nigerian track and field teams have medaled in international games, including winning the gold medal in the 4 x 100 men's relay in the 1992 Summer Olympics in Barcelona, and silver medals at the 1996 and 2000 Summer Olympic Games in Atlanta and Sidney, Australia. But over the years the most medals have been won by Nigerian boxers.

Senegal and Nigeria face off in the African Cup quarterfinals in soccer, Nigeria's favorite sport.

Nigerian athletes participate in all kinds of sports both in Nigeria and around the world. There are local and national clubs and training facilities all over the country. At school, children participate in all kinds of sports with the dream of becoming professional athletes.

THE EDUCATIONAL SYSTEM

In addition to offering a wide variety of recreational and sports activities, Nigeria has a strong educational system, at least in comparison to other African countries. In the 1990s, the country instituted what is known as a 6-3-3-4 system, modeled after the U.S. system. Education consists of six years of primary school, three years of junior secondary school, three years of senior secondary (high) school, and four years or more of college. Preschool and kindergarten are not required; but some parents who can afford it send their children to private preschools and kindergartens. Elementary schools are day schools, but at the junior and senior high school levels, students may choose between a boarding school or a day school. Boarding schools are very popular because they give students the opportunity to leave home for a period of time. There are also vocational training schools for those who do not want to attend secondary schools.

In 1970, Nigeria instituted a policy of universal free education for primary schools. This was aimed at encouraging families to send their children to school, and the goal is to achieve 100 percent primary school enrollment by the year 2010. In the year 2000, about 88 percent of eligible students were enrolled in the nation's primary schools. However, the number falls drastically at the secondary level because, unlike primary education, secondary education is not free. This means that parents who want their children to go to secondary school have to find ways to fund it; this is difficult, and often impossible, for parents from poor families.

Entrance exams are taken at each level of schooling to determine a student's eligibility to move on to the next level. All the exams are national and are administered by agencies other than the local schools. This creates some accountability and uniformity in the school system.

A variation in the uniformity occurs in the northern region, where children may receive Koranic instruction in addition to their Western education. In Koranic schools,

LIFE IN A BOARDING SCHOOL

A number of Nigerian secondary school students attend boarding schools. Many students prefer boarding schools to day schools because it gives them the opportunity to leave home for a period of time. Life at these schools is very structured. John Owhonda describes an ordinary day at boarding school in his book *Nigeria: A Nation of Many Peoples*.

A typical day at most Nigerian secondary schools begins at 5:30 A.M. when the rising, or wake-up, bell is rung. It is still a bit dark outside, and the roosters are just crowing as students make their beds. At 6:00 A.M. the students troop out to appointed areas for morning chores. Some may pick up fallen leaves, sweep the schoolyard and playgrounds, or tend the garden. Others may wash the bathrooms. At 6:30, all must shower and dress for classes. Breakfast is at 7:00, and classes begin an hour later.

Lunch is at 2:00 P.M., followed by a siesta, or afternoon nap, or rest, required of all students. Siesta lasts an hour and a half. Sports and games begin at 4:30 in the afternoon. Everyone must take part, either as a player in such sports as soccer, lawn tennis, and basketball or as a spectator of other sporting events such as table tennis and track and field.

Dinner is served at 6:00 P.M. Afterward, the students report to their classrooms to do homework assignments in preparation for the next day's classes. Students are not allowed to talk or wander around during this time. Prep classes end at 9:30, and students are in bed by 10. Although the routine at Nigeria's secondary schools may sound like that of a military academy, Nigerian students enjoy the responsibility and fun of living and studying in boarding schools with hundreds of their peers.

students are taught the Arabic language and Islamic principles. Except in the schools where Arabic is taught, English is the official language of instruction. Other languages, including French, German, and indigenous languages, are taught as special subjects. This is why most educated Nigerians are bilingual, speaking and writing English as well as their native language.

Children in both primary and secondary schools are required to wear school uniforms. Often, the uniforms consist

These children attend a Koranic school, where they learn Islamic principles as well as receive a Western education.

of a white shirt and skirt or pinafore of another color for girls and a white shirt with pants or shorts for boys. Everybody is expected to wear brown sandals or white canvas shoes. Girls wear their hair short or have it neatly braided, depending on the school. Boys always wear their hair short. At both primary and secondary levels, children walk the distance to and from school because there are no school buses. The school year runs from January to December; there are three terms with a month-long break between each.

After students complete secondary school, there are many institutions of higher learning, such as universities, polytechnics, colleges of science and technology, teacher training colleges, and nursing schools, for those who want to further their education. Nigeria boasts a high number of university graduates, but not everyone who wishes to attend institutions of higher learning can. Even someone who passes the required entrance examinations can still be denied admission to college. This is because, even though Nigeria has many institutions of higher learning, it does not have enough spaces to accommodate every student. In 1998, only about 20 percent of students seeking higher education could be enrolled. Bello Ahmad Salim, an education official, says that "during the 1996/7 school year, only 79,904 were offered places in the universities by the board from the pool of 475,923 students who applied for places."[5]

From the villages to the cities, life in Nigeria is vibrant, offering a blend of old values and new emerging ways. But, like most developing countries, Nigeria faces the challenge of meeting the economic needs of its people. It must raise the standard of living, especially in the rural areas, and ensure that all those who aspire to further their education are able to do so. The future of the nation depends on its ability to meet the needs of its people.

6
Nigeria's Cultural and Literary Legacy

Despite, or perhaps because of, Nigeria's political and economic problems, its people have always thrived in the areas of visual arts and literature. Historically, the people's art chronicled their heritage, revealing their practical and spiritual views of life. Today Nigeria's art continues the legacy of the past, yet incorporates a modern attitude that reflects contemporary concerns and modes of thought. Nigeria's art and literature are unique for both their comprehensiveness and versatility, and they have made a lasting cultural impact in Africa and the rest of the world.

The Visual Arts

The word that best describes Nigerian visual art is *variety*. The work of Nigerian visual artists exhibits fine workmanship and great skills, and spans all aspects of life, from spiritual to secular. Art ranges from the abstract to more realistic depictions, depending on the artist's individual preference and convictions. Taken together, Nigerian art speaks of the people's values, their attitudes toward life, and events in their history. The works include sculptures, weavings, carvings, pottery, and metalwork.

Sculpture

The oldest surviving Nigerian art comes from the Nok people, who lived in the present-day Jos area from 500 to 200 B.C. Their work consists of terra-cotta sculptures that vary in size from miniature figures only a few inches high to larger-than-life figures. The sculptures offer stylized interpretations of natural forms, especially the human form. Hairstyles and ornaments and facial features are carefully detailed.

The Ife bronzes, which date from the thirteenth century A.D., more than a thousand years after the terra-cottas of the Nok people, provide a glimpse into another prominent ancient Nigerian culture. The Ife bronzes are products of the period when the Yoruba kingdom of Ife flourished. They systematically chronicle the lives of the different *onis* (kings) of the kingdom, and the best-known works are artistic portraits of the court personalities who lived so long ago. Pierre Meauze, curator of the Museum of African Arts in Paris, writes in his book *African Art*, "every time we contemplate a magnificent Ife bronze mask, we realize that it will always retain its rightful place, immovable in its detached serenity."[6]

Like the Ife bronzes, the Benin brass plates and bronzes that date from the fifteenth century, when the kingdom of Benin ruled the land, depict the court culture of the time, and provide many details of dress, weapons, and ceremonial instruments. Some of the works chronicle the invasion of the land by the Portuguese during the fifteenth century. The details in these works—big beards, long noses, quilted dress, crossbows, and muskets—emphasize the appearance of the Portuguese. The craftsmanship of the Nok, Ife, and Benin sculptures emanates power and reveals much of past times. This is why they still capture people's attention and imagination today. The works are showcased in many museums in Nigeria, other African countries, and the Western world.

Modern sculptors carry on the fine craftsmanship of their ancestors, but present contemporary interpretations of life. There are many artists' guilds all over Nigeria through which individuals produce and showcase their work. Unlike the Nok, Ife, and Benin bronzes, which are very realistic, the works of some Nigerian artists deal in the world of the abstract. These pieces add yet another dimension to Nigerian art collections.

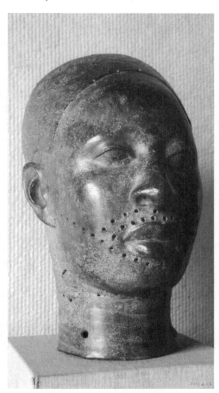

This Ife bronze head belongs to a collection of sculptures that chronicled the lives of Nigerian kings beginning in the thirteenth century.

WOODWORK

Like sculpture, woodworking is an art that has a long history in Nigeria. Most of the woodwork that have survived from the past is not court art like the Ife and Benin bronzes; instead, they depict ordinary people living ordinary lives. The oldest surviving carvings are the Oron wood carvings found in the Niger Delta area. These full-size figures are believed to represent leaders of the towns and villages.

Today carving is often a family trade, and sons are trained to take over the work from their fathers. Carvings are practical as well as ornamental. Many houses are adorned with carved doors, furniture, and wooden ornamental staffs and bowls. Carved masks used in festivals are also popular, and many have religious meanings because they depict the faces of the gods being honored during the festivals. Other religious works include carved images of the cult of ancestors used in traditional African worship, and carvings of the personal gods that people carry with them to ward off evil spirits.

Carving calabashes is common among the Yorubas and the Hausas. Calabashes are gourds that grow on trees usually found in the drier regions of central and northern Nigeria. The gourds have different sizes and shapes. Artists harvest mature gourds, clean them and allow them to dry, then carve and paint different colorful designs on them. The finished calabashes have many uses, both practical and ornamental. Some are used as dishes; others are used to add finishing

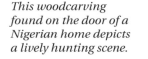

This woodcarving found on the door of a Nigerian home depicts a lively hunting scene.

A merchant displays an extensive variety of multicolored cloths and weavings made from local yarns and dyes.

touches to interior decorations; and rounded ones are used as colorful musical instruments, with beads attached.

WEAVING

Weaving is as ancient as sculpture and carving in Nigeria. Nigerian men and women weave cloths as well as mats of various designs from local materials. In the north, cloth weaving is often the work of men. The city of Kano was famous for its cloth as early as the thirteenth century A.D. In the south, the Yorubas and the Ibos weave the Ashoke and the Akwete cloth. These strong cloths are multicolored and made from locally spun yarns and dyes. The Akwete and Ashoke are in great demand among the upper-crust Nigerians and foreign tourists because of their limited production and fine workmanship. The Ijebu women of Yorubaland are also known for their speciality in tie-dying.

Mats of various lengths and designs are made from special plants and the fiber of raffia palms that grow in abundance throughout the coastal region. The mats are used both for decoration and for practical purposes like sleeping and sitting. In the north, worshipers kneel on the mats during daily prayers at home and in the mosques.

LITERATURE

Like that of its visual arts, Nigeria's literary history is rich and extensive. Long before they began to use writing, Nigerians wove tales about their lives and passed them orally to younger generations. Storytelling was an integral aspect of life. Myths, legends, and folklore chronicled the people's history and preserved their identity and values. Today, now that many Nigerian languages have been rendered into writing, Nigerian authors carry on the work of their ancestors, weaving tales of contemporary life with their pens. However, oral tradition still remains a vibrant component of social life.

ORAL LITERATURE

The Nigerian oral tradition is rich in proverbs, poetry, and folklore. As in many African communities, proverbs feature prominently in social and political settings. Every man or woman of importance is expected to know how to use proverbs. The proverbs express ages of proven wisdom and are used to instruct as well as to invoke shared values. It would be difficult to attend a meeting of elders and not be astounded by the number of proverbs used. Sometimes entire conversations are carried on in proverbs, as people greatly versed in the art of speaking show off their skills. To Westerners, the use of proverbs may seem like a roundabout way of making a point. But among Africans, bluntness is not considered a virtue, and proverbs are used to communicate but not appear overtly aggressive, an asset when dealing with difficult and provocative issues.

Like the use of proverbs, oral poetry is an integral part of life. Most of the poems appear as songs, which are sung for every occasion. These songs include dirges, praise songs, and songs for birth ceremonies. Some are formal and are composed by paid court or village poets; others are informal, spontaneous songs that result from the spirit of the occasion. Either way, the poems are full of intricate images that reveal aspects of the people's philosophies of life as well as their experiences. For example, in the poem "Hunger," the anonymous poet makes the point that hunger is a dominating human experience. When a person is hungry, nothing else matters until that hunger is satisfied:

Hunger makes a person lie down—
He has water in his knees.
Hunger makes a person lie down
And count the rafters in his roof.
When the Muslim is not hungry he says:
We are forbidden to eat monkey.
When he is hungry he eats a baboon.
Hunger will drive the Muslim woman from the harem
Out into the street,
Hunger will persuade the priest
To steal from his own shrine.
"I have eaten yesterday"
Does not concern hunger.
There is no god like one's stomach:
We must sacrifice to it every day.[7]

Poems like "Hunger" that give insights into specific aspects of daily life are popular, and so are praise songs. The Yorubas and the Hausas are particularly known for their praise songs. Praise songs grew out of the monarchical systems. Troubadours composed on-the-spot songs in praise of the kings in the hope of being showered with gifts. These songs often included a eulogy of the family lineage, tracing the great deeds of the king's forefathers and showing how the king fulfills his role as the champion of the people.

Coronation ceremonies would be incomplete without praise songs, composed by a chosen court poet. These poems are often the highlight of the ceremony, for they remind the people not only of the deeds of former kings but of their collective history as a people. Those commissioned to compose praise songs for community events spend months at their work, as the task is taken seriously. Praise songs are usually accompanied by musical instruments such as gongs, drums, and, for special celebrations, bagpipes. Oral poetry in Nigeria is anonymous, and even when the original poets are known, people are free to use and modify the poems as they see fit. There is no copyright law.

FOLKLORE

Similar to oral poetry, myths, legends, and folktales trace the history of the people and express their values. They serve as great preservers and chroniclers of the people's heritage. The tales are told during community events by trained story-tellers. But at the heart of the genre are the tales that parents tell their young children around campfires or fireplaces. At night, when all the chores are done, Nigerian children might sit around the hearth and listen to their father tell stories, stories that have been passed down for generations. On rainy summer days, some families roast home-grown corn in the fire and feast on the roasted corn, coconuts, and African pears as they listen to the tales.

Many of the folk stories are about the adventures of the turtle, the trickster in most Nigerian folktales. The stories are meant not only to entertain the listener but to transmit communal values. In each, there is a lesson that, if applied, would help a person live a useful life. Folktales are easy to remember because they evoke memorable images and feelings.

THE *OBA* OF BENIN

Nigerian folk poetry contains many praise poems, like this one by an anonymous author in U11i Beier's *African Poetry.*

> He who knows not the Oba
> let me show him.
> He has mounted the throne,
> he has piled a throne upon a throne.
> Plentiful as grains of sand on the earth
> are those in front of him.
> Plentiful as grains of sand on the earth
> are those behind him.
> There are two thousand people
> to fan him.
> He who owns you
> is among you here.
> He who owns you
> has piled a throne upon throne.
> He has lived to do it this year;
> even so he will to do it again.

Recognizing the power of folktales in community life, many contemporary writers weave them into their plots. For example, Chinua Achebe, an internationally known Nigerian author, makes one of his characters in *Things Fall Apart* tell a folktale. This enables him to comment on the value of such tales in the lives of the family and the community.

WRITTEN LITERATURE

Contemporary Nigerian written literature covers a variety of genres, from poetic and dramatic works to nonfiction and fiction. Some authors, such as J. P. Clark, focus on shared native experiences, beliefs, and customs. Others, such as Amos Tutuola, show the influence of Western thought and its intrusion upon the lives of the people. Tutuola's most well-known novel, *The Palm Wine Drinkard*, is a work that fuses popular folktales into a continuous narration centered around a main character. The quest that the major character takes to gain knowledge of the world expresses the Yoruba concept of the spirit world and its relationship to the familiar world of human experiences. The book also reflects the Western influence in Nigeria during the 1950s, when the novel was first published.

Other Nigerian writers as Chinua Achebe and Wole Soyinka focus on British colonization and its impact on Nigerian politics and culture. Chinua Achebe, in *Things Fall Apart*, blames the British for failing to understand the indigenous culture of the people they colonized, and consequently destroying what was good within traditional institutions in the name of bringing so-called civilization to Nigerians. The book's title itself suggests that things fell apart for Nigerians when the British brought their Western values to the land and began forcing the people to adopt them. *Things Fall Apart* is still considered revolutionary in African literature because it was the first novel to show the negative impact that colonization had on the African people. It is taught in many classrooms around the world and has been translated into many languages.

Like Achebe, Obikaram Echewa draws on Nigeria's colonial history in his book *I Saw the Sky Catch Fire*. This novel imaginatively depicts the famous Aba Women's Riot in which a group of women in southeastern Nigeria tried to resist the British political and social imposition at the turn of the twentieth

ABIKU

Some contemporary Nigerian authors explore native beliefs and values in their work. In his poem "Abiku," (found in *The Heinemann Book of African Poetry in English*), poet J. P. Clark explores one aspect of the African concept of reincarnation. The Abiku concept is the African belief that some children, out of some supernatural phenomenon, are born several times in a lifetime to the same woman. The children are born and die over and over until a ritual is performed to stop them from torturing the mother.

Coming and going these several seasons
Do stay out on the baobab tree,
Follow where you please your kindred spirits
If indoors is not enough for you.
True, it leaks through the thatch
When floods brim the banks,
And the bats and the owls
Often tear in at night through the eaves,
And at harmattan, the bamboo walls
Are ready tinder for the fire
That dries the fresh fish up on the rack.
Still, it's been the healthy stock
To several fingers, to many more will be
Who reach to the sun,
No longer then bestride the threshold
But step in and stay
For good. We know the knife scars
Serrating down your back and front
Like the beak of the sword-fish,
And both your ears, notched
As a bondman to this house,
Are all relics for your first comings.
Then stop in, step in and stay,
For her body is tired,
Tired, her milk going sour
Where many more mouths gladden the heart.

century. The works of female writers such as Flora Nwapa and Buchi Emecheta also confront issues concerning Nigerian women.

In recent years, the emphasis in literature has shifted from colonial life to more contemporary issues. Recent writings have focused on the political and social instabilities in the country. But whether their subject is about life during colonial rule or life in recent times, many Nigerian writers find audiences around the world. Their works are regularly read and studied in secondary schools and universities. In 1986, Wole Soyinka, a Nigerian novelist and playwright, was awarded the Nobel Prize for literature. He was the first African to be given the honor, which many felt was overdue.

MUSIC

Not only is music as integral to Nigerian life as storytelling, it seems to dominate all aspects of life, political, social, and religious. One can hardly walk down the street anywhere in Nigeria without being exposed to one kind of music or another. There are songs to welcome a newborn, songs for puberty, songs for weddings, burial songs, church music, and secular music. Nigeria is home to many internationally known musicians, including Sunny Ade, Sonny Okosun, Fela Kuti, Sade, Joni Haastrup, Prince Niko, and Chief Osadebe. Most of the musicians live in Nigeria, many in Lagos, the music capital of the country, but travel all over the world with their music. Others live outside Nigeria.

Contemporary secular music comes in many forms—the Afro-beat, juju, the high-life, and the African blues. These combine traditional instruments and styles with contemporary ones. The juju, for example, integrates Yoruba traditional and folk music with modern African styles. All Nigerian music, secular or otherwise, is polyrhythmic, which is why it would be difficult to sit still while listening to any good Nigerian music. The songs are accompanied by many instruments, especially the African talking drums responsible for the music's characteristic high-energy tempo.

Nigerian musicians are multilingual, singing in English and many native languages as well as pidgin or creole English. One recording may contain the same song in many languages or feature different parts of one song performed in many languages. The sound and the lyrics of the songs are considered equally important. The sound energizes and draws in the listener, and the lyrics express shared thoughts and values. It is in this sense that music serves to educate, to question, and to embody the collective voices and experiences of the people.

The themes and styles of Nigerian music vary immensely, even in the work of one musician. Some, like Sonny Okosun, deplore what they see as the plundering of Nigerian wealth by its leaders. His songs such as "Power to the People" and "Papa's Land" are political; he refers to them as "songs for people to think about."[8] In his most popular song, "Which Way Nigeria?" he asked the essential question on the minds of many Nigerians in the early 1980s when the government seemed incapable of running the country. Other musicians, especially those living in the West, have a different focus. Joni

Popular musician Sunny Ade performs in concert.

JUJU MUSIC

One of the many types of music produced by Nigerian musicians is juju music. In his book *Africa O-Ye! A Celebration of African Music*, Graeme Ewens discusses the historical value of the music to Nigerians, especially people from the Yoruba ethnic group, where juju music is said to have originated.

The fluid interplay between talking drums, wailing Hawaiian style electric guitar, and call-and-response vocals which characterizes juju music heralds one of the most successful of the continent's uni-cultural or "tribal" music. Juju is a contemporary social music which also incorporates several cultural functions, including praise singing and worship, or acknowledgment, of both Christian and Yoruba values.

The idea of gods and juju conjures images of strangeness which would have inspired fear in White breasts a few generations ago. "The name juju music is a name given to the particular music by the colonial people," said Sunny Ade, the so-called King of juju. "In the old days any Black (African) medicine was called juju and any music playing around there, they called it juju music. But now it is a different music entirely and we still want the name to remain. Because it is a name which is simple to call, like rock, jazz, reggae, soul, juju that is the name of the music. The meaning of juju is not connected to Black medicine or magic or anything like that." Traditional Yoruba culture is rich . . . and a particular Yoruba characteristic is the ability to incorporate new and alien elements into their own culture, and juju has been the musical form to be most spectacularly modernized throughout its history.

Haastrup's dream is to be known simply as an artist, not just an African musician. Babatunde Olatunji, based in California, sees himself as the ambassador of African culture. He has attempted to correct America's misconceptions of Africa and has fought to protect African traditions from Western cultural dominance. To see his troupe of drummers and dancers is to "experience the uninhibited exuberance and excitement of Africa,"[9] says writer Gary Stewart.

There is no question that Nigerian musicians have had and continue to have a lasting influence on Western musicians.

VICTOR UWAIFO, THE GUITAR BOY

Nigeria has many musicians whose impact has been felt in both the local and the international scene. In his book *West African Pop Roots*, John Collins discusses the achievements of Victor Uwaifo, one of Nigeria's preeminent musicians.

Victor Uwaifo is one of the most dynamic African musicians. He has released over one hundred singles and a dozen albums since he formed his Melody Maestros in 1965. His music has a driving beat based on the local folk music from the Bendel state of Nigeria, merged with a modern touch. It all started in 1966 when he and his band released smash hits on the Phonogram label. These singles were "Sirir-Sirri," "Joromi," and "Guitar-boy." "Joromi," based on the story of a legendary hero of Benin City, was so popular that it earned Uwaifo Africa's first Gold Disc Award in 1969. "Joromi" also became the name for one of the bright African cloth designs. Since then, Victor has become so famous that the students of the University of Nigeria, Nsukka knighted him "Sir" Victor Uwaifo, a name that has stayed with him ever since. The Melody Maestros have made many international tours. They represented Nigeria at the Black Arts Festival in Dakar in 1966, and played at the Algerian Arts Expo in 1969 and the 1970 World Expo in Japan. They have also toured in the United States, Europe, and Russia.

Mickey Hart of the Grateful Dead collaborated with Babatunde Olatunji, dubbed Nigeria's master drummer, for his albums *Dance to the Beat of My Drum* (later rereleased as *Drums of Passions: The Beat*) and *Drums of Passions: The Invocation*. Hart says of Olatunji, "He was the first one that I heard use the talking drums or variable pitched drums in his performance, you know, in African performance. And he mixed the African performance with the urban New York music. And it was the combination, brass and percussion and voice, that changed the way I thought about drums."[10]

THE PERFORMING ARTS

The newest arrivals to the Nigerian arts scene are the performing arts. Nigerian life, however, has always been full of drama. During festivals, dancers and masquerades depicted different aspects of traditional life, relationships between humans and the gods, and people's relationship to the natural world. Storytellers performed their stories and aroused the people's emotions through songs and gestures. Today, even though dramatic storytelling is still an integral aspect of community life, performances have evolved to include formal plays staged in community and regional theaters.

The coming of the media age has added another dimension to the arts in Nigeria. Until the middle of the 1980s, most of the films in Nigeria were foreign films with foreign themes. Often, because many people did not understand the themes, the cinema was considered outside the realm of ordinary Nigerians. But in recent years Nigerian-based screenwriters have been producing films featuring Nigerian themes, which are gaining wide audiences. Like traditional storytelling and plays, most of the movies and shows impart moral lessons. Television is also popular, and shows range from comedies to religious dramas to soap operas.

Taken altogether, Nigerian arts and literature offer an immense variety of themes and styles. They combine the traditional and the contemporary to represent a culture that is rich in history and human potential. As the new generation of artists sustain and extend the vision of their elders, there is no question that Nigeria will remain a viable center for visual arts, music, and literature in the international community.

EPILOGUE

AFRICA'S GIANT

The size of its population, its economic resources, and, ironically, its political troubles have combined to make Nigeria a leader in Africa. To many Africans, Nigeria is fondly viewed as the "big brother," a reference to the idea that other nations look to Nigeria for leadership in the international community. There seems to be a feeling that the internal political problems of Nigeria are not unlike those facing other African nations and that if Nigeria can make it, others can also. During his trip to Nigeria in August 2000, U.S. president Bill Clinton commented, "Nigeria and the transition there is of huge importance. Given its size and its potential role in stabilizing and democratizing Africa, Nigeria represents a huge opportunity for our interests in Africa and also a challenge."[11]

Nigeria recognizes its role and potential role in the international community. Throughout its various administrations, Nigeria has been committed to the independence and unity of all African states. It is a founding member of many organizations aimed at establishing African solidarity, including the Organization of African Unity (OAU) and the Economic Community of West African States (ECOWAS), which seeks to harmonize trade and investment practices for its sixteen West African members. Nigeria is also a member of the Non-aligned Movement and the United Nations.

NIGERIA'S LEADERSHIP

Nigeria played a role in helping Zimbabwe and, later, Namibia gain independence in the 1980s. It was a leading voice in condemning apartheid and in encouraging the imposition of economic sanctions on South Africa. These sanctions eventually pressured South African leaders into dismantling apartheid in favor of a democratic political process that includes blacks in the running of their own country.

Nigeria has also played a leading role in ending disputes and internal wars in many African nations. It has taken part in peacekeeping forces to Chad, Somalia, Liberia, and Sierra

Leone. The bulk of the ECOMOG (Economic Community Cease-fire Monitoring Group) peacekeeping troops in Liberia and Sierra Leone were from Nigeria. As Joseph P. Smaldone states, "Since independence, Nigeria has proudly boasted Africa's longest and most distinguished record of participation in United Nations' peace keeping operations."[12] Nigeria in most cases has borne the financial burden of these peacekeeping missions, and many Nigerian peacekeepers have lost their lives, but the nation's commitment remains strong.

Internally, Nigeria's social, economic, and political problems may seem daunting, and from time to time the people may lose faith in their leaders and their abilities to help themselves. But they also recognize that with understanding and commitment, the country's problems are not insurmountable. With the right kind of leaders and the help of its enormous human and economic resources, Nigeria could once again rise to meet the needs of its peoples. In many ways, Nigeria has the potential of being one of the most effective nations in the world.

While other African nations look to Nigeria for leadership in the international community, its expansion in human and natural resources continues.

Facts About Nigeria

Government

Type: Multiparty government (democratic).

1914–1960: Under colonial rule.

1960–1963: Parliamentary system of government.

1963–1966: Federal system of government.

1966–1979: Military rule.

1979–1983: Civilian rule.

1983–1999: Military rule.

1999–Present: Civilian rule.

Date of Independence

October 1, 1960.

National Holidays

January 1: New Year's Day.

January 19: Id al-Fitr, end of Ramadan.

March 28: Id al-Kabir, Feast of Sacrifice.

March/April: Easter.

June 26: Birth of the Prophet.

October 1: Independence Day.

November/December: Ramadan.

December 25: Christmas Day.

December 26: Boxing Day.

People

Population (2000 est.): 113,000,000.

Capital: Abuja (339,000, 1995 est.).

Languages: English (official), Yoruba, Ibo, Hausa, and more than four hundred others.

Ethnicities: Hausa, Fulani, Yoruba, Ibo, Bini, Ibibio, Tiv, Ijaw, Kanuri, and many others.

Religion: Christian, 45 percent; Islam, 45 percent; indigenous, 10 percent.

Literacy rate: 51 percent (1990 est.).

Education: Primary attendance, 80 percent; secondary attendance, 50 percent.

Workforce: 42.844 million; agriculture, 54 percent; industry and commerce, 19 percent; government, 15 percent; other, 12 percent.

Life expectancy: Males, 55 years; females, 57 years.

Infant mortality: 70 deaths per 1,000 births.

Population density: 480 per square mile.

Annual population growth: 2.6 percent.

GEOGRAPHY

Area: 356,700 square miles.

Coastline: 530 miles.

ECONOMY

Currency: Naira.

Inflation rate: 15 percent.

Unemployment rate: 28 percent.

Exports: Petroleum and petroleum-related products, cocoa, and rubber.

Imports: Manufactured goods, machines, food products, chemicals, and transportation equipment.

Natural resources: Petroleum, tin, columbite, iron ore, limestone, lead, coal, zinc, and natural gas.

CHRONOLOGY

500 B.C.
Nok culture is established in Nigeria.

700 A.D.
Igbo Ukwu culture is established in Nigeria.

1000–1100
Hausa communities are established in northern and southern Nigeria.

1200–1500
The Benin empire is established.

1300
The Oyo empire is established.

1350
Hausa city-states emerge.

1400s
Islam is introduced to Hausaland by the Mandigo people from Senegal.

1471
The Portuguese land on the Niger and visit the Benin empire.

1510
The slave trade begins.

1804
Othman Dan Fodio begins his jihad; the Netherlands ban the slave trade for its citizens.

1807
Britain bans the slave trade for its citizens.

1808
The United States bans the importation of slaves.

1809
Hausa city chiefs are defeated by Dan Fodio and his followers; the Sokoto empire is founded.

1830
Sokoto reaches its greatest extent.

1836
The Oyo empire dissolves.

1884–1885
At the Berlin Conference, Africa is partitioned among rival European nations.

1903
Sokoto is conquered by the British.

1914
The Southern and Northern Protectorates join to form Nigeria.

1950s
Petroleum is discovered around the Niger Delta.

October 1, 1960
Nigeria achieves independence from Britain.

January 1966
First military coup; General Aguiyi Ironsi becomes commander-in-chief of the nation.

July 1966
Countercoup; General Yakubu Gowon takes over the government; Ironsi is assassinated.

May 1967
The Ibos declare their independence and secession from the federation.

1967–1970
The civil war, also called the Nigerian-Biafran War.

1975–1998
Nigeria is controlled by a series of short-lived military and civilian governments.

June 8, 1998
Head of state Sani Abacha dies of a heart attack; General Abdulsalami Abubakar becomes head of state.

December 1998–January 1999
Olusegun Obasanjo is elected president of the republic.

May 1999
The new civilian leaders are inaugurated.

Notes

Introduction: Nigeria A Complex Society

1. Michael Crowder, *A Short History of Nigeria*. New York: Frederick A. Praeger, 1962, p. 20.

2. Special report, *New York Times*, August 20, 2000, p. A1.

Chapter 3: Contact with Europe

3. Quoted in Helen Chapin Metz, ed., *Nigeria: A Country Study*. Washington, DC: Federal Research Division, 1992, p. 56.

Chapter 4: Nigerian Government and Politics

4. Stella Nwaru, interview with the author, Richmond, Kentucky, September 2000.

Chapter 5: Everyday life

5. Quoted in "Education" page, wwww.motherlandnigeria.com/education.

Chapter 6: Nigeria's Cultural and Literary Legacy

6. Pierre Meauze, *African Art*. New York: Arch Cape Press, 1991, p. 14.

7. Quoted in Ruth Finnegan, ed., *A World Treasury of Oral Poetry*. Bloomington: Indiana University Press, 1978, p. 166.

8. Quoted in Gary Stewart, *Breakout: Profiles in African Rhythm*. Chicago: University of Chicago Press, 1992, p. 88.

9. Stewart, *Breakout*, p. 88.

10. Quoted in Stewart, *Breakout*, p. 88.

Epilogue: Africa's Giant

11. Quoted in Norimitsu Onishi, "Against Tough Odds, Nigeria Bets on Reform," *New York Times*, August 20, 2000, p. 18.

12. Quoted in Metz, *Nigeria*, p. 268.

SUGGESTIONS FOR FURTHER READING

Diagram Group, *Peoples of West Africa*. New York: Facts On File, 1997. Gives an overview of every major ethnic group in West Africa.

Kim Elliott, *Benin: An African Kingdom and Culture*. Minneapolis: Lerner Publications, 1979. An informed overview of the Benin culture and empire.

Ekpo Eyo and Frank Willett, *Treasure of Ancient Nigeria*. New York: Alfred A. Knopf, 1980. Photographs and text offer a historical discussion of Nigerian art.

Nicholas Frevile, *Nigeria*. Philadelphia: Chelsea House, 2000. Photographs and text look at the past development and present culture of Nigeria and its peoples.

Ifeoma Onyefulu, *Ebele's Favorite: A Book of African Games*. London: Frances Lincoln, 1999. Offers colorful illustrations of how to play many African games.

John Owhonda, *Nigeria: A Nation of Many Peoples*. Parsippany, NJ: Dillion Press, 1998. An exciting and easy-to-read book on various aspects of Nigerian culture and history.

John Peffer-Engels, *The Benin Kingdom of West Africa*. Boulder, CO: Netlibrary, 1996. A good account of the historic kingdom of Benin in Nigeria.

Anne Rosenberg, *Nigeria: The Culture*. New York: Crabtree, 2000. A description of the culture of the various peoples of Nigeria, with pictures.

———, *Nigeria: The People*. New York: Crabtree, 2000. A description of the peoples of Nigeria, with pictures.

WORKS CONSULTED

BOOKS

J. F. A. Ajayi, *Milestones in Nigerian History*. London: Longman, 1980. Reviews important dates in Nigerian history.

Ulli Beier, ed., *African Poetry*. Cambridge, England: Cambridge University Press, 1966. A collection of oral poetry from several African ethnic groups.

Harm J. de Blij, *A Geography of Sub-Saharan Africa*. Chicago: Rand McNally, 1964. Description of the vegetation and physical features of the geographic regions of sub-Saharan Africa.

Alan Burns, *History of Nigeria*. London: George Allen and Unwin, 1963. A good book on the European colonial activities in Nigeria.

John Collins, *West African Pop Roots*. Philadelphia: Temple University Press, 1992. A detailed overview of the history of African popular music.

Michael Crowder, *A Short History of Nigeria*. New York: Praeger, 1962. A very useful book that details the history of Nigeria from precolonial times to independence.

Graeme Ewens, *Africa O-Ye! A Celebration of African Music*. New York: Guinness, 1991. Good discussion of the African music industry.

Ruth Finnegan, ed., *A World Treasury of Oral Poetry*. Bloomington: Indiana University Press, 1978. A collection of oral poetry from many world cultures.

Jean Herskovits, *Nigeria: Power and Democracy in Africa*. New York: Foreign Policy Association Headline Series, 1982. Gives a brief overview of the history of Nigerian politics.

H. A. S. Johnston, *The Fulani Empire of Sokoto*. London: Oxford University Press, 1967. Gives a historical account of the Fulani ethnic group in Nigeria.

101

Colin Latchem, *Looking at Nigeria.* Philadelphia: Lippincott, 1975. Gives a brief overview of the history, geography, and peoples of Nigeria.

Colin Legum, ed., *Africa: A Handbook.* New York: Praeger, 1966. Contains many essays on different issues in Africa, from politics to literature.

Adewale Maja-Pearce, ed., *The Heinemann Book of African Poetry in English.* London: Heinemann, 1990. A collection of poems from several African writers.

Pierre Meauze, *African Art.* New York: Arch Cape Press, 1991. Offers an informed discussion of the different types of Nigerian sculptures and their historical significance; also contains photographs of the sculptures discussed.

Helen Chapin Metz, ed., *Nigeria: A Country Study.* Washington, DC: Federal Research Division, 1992. An overview of the historical, economic, social, and political aspects of Nigeria.

John Middleton, *Peoples of Africa.* New York: Arco, 1978. Gives a good overview of the history and way of life of many ethnic groups in Africa.

Lois Mitchison, *Nigeria: Newest Nation.* New York: Praeger, 1960. Gives a historical and political account of Nigeria right before its independence in 1960.

Richard Olaniyan, ed., *Nigerian History and Culture.* Hong Kong: Longman, 1985. Gives an informed discussion of the many events that led to the Nigerian civil war and the aftermath of the war.

Gary Stewart, *Breakout: Profiles in African Rhythm.* Chicago: University of Chicago Press, 1992. Profiles major African musicians.

Reuben K. Udo, *Geographic Regions of Nigeria.* Berkeley and Los Angeles: University of California Press, 1970. Offers a very detailed description of the many geographic zones in Nigeria.

Andre Viola, Jacqueline Bardolph, and Denise Coussy, *New Fiction in English from Africa.* Atlanta: 1998. Gives scholarly reviews of major African writers and their contributions to modern African fiction.

Christopher Alan Waterman, *Juju*, Chicago: University of Chicago Press, 1990. Gives a social history of the African popular music.

PERIODICALS

Christian Science Monitor, "Nigerian Girl to Be Lashed 180 Times," January 4, 2001.

Christianity Today, "Will Shari'a Law Curb Christianity?" October 23, 2000.

Economist, "Nigeria's Democracy Dividend," December 16, 2000.

Ronald Miller, "The Climate of Nigeria," *Geography: A Journal of Geographical Association*, 1952, vol. 37.

Norimitsu Onishi, "Against Tough Odds, Nigeria Bets on Reform," *New York Times*, August 20, 2000.

WEBSITES

Motherland Nigeria (www.motherlandnigeria.com). This is an award-winning website that offers an overview of different aspects of life in Nigeria. The website is continuously updated to accommodate the developments in Nigerian political and social life. It also gives brief biographies of prominent Nigerians and links searchers to other websites on Nigeria.

"Nigeria: Background Notes on Countries of the World" (www.odci.gov/cia/publications/factbook/ni.html). This information on Nigeria formally produced in print by the U.S. government is now available on-line. It still gives the most up-to-date brief overviews and data on every aspect of Nigerian life.

NigeriaNews (www.Nigerianews.net). Offers information on daily events in Nigeria. Updated daily.

NigeriaWEB Documents (http://odili.net). Provides many documents on Nigeria, including full texts of speeches given by Nigerian politicians and the full text of the 1999 Nigerian constitution.

INDEX

PICTURE CREDITS

About the Author

Salome Nnoromele is a native of Nigeria. She received her undregraduate degree from the University of Utah in Salt Lake City. Her master's and doctorate degrees are from the University of Kentucky. She is currently an associate professor of English at Eastern Kentucky University. She is also the author of two other books for Lucent Books and several essays on African culture and literature.